THE BRITISH MUSEUM CONCISE INTRODUCTION TO
ANCIENT ROME

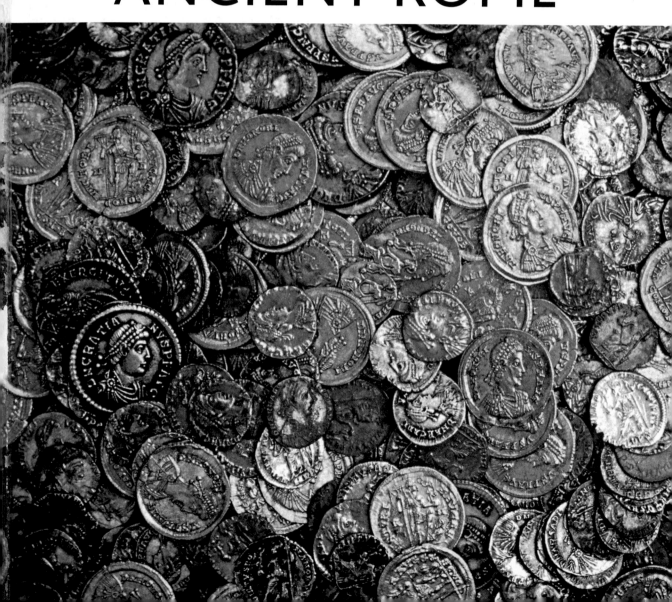

THE BRITISH MUSEUM CONCISE INTRODUCTION TO
ANCIENT ROME
NANCY H. RAMAGE & ANDREW RAMAGE

THE UNIVERSITY OF MICHIGAN PRESS

ANN ARBOR

2011 2010 2009 2008   4 3 2 1

Library of Congress Cataloging-in-Publication Data

Ramage, Nancy H., 1942–
      The British Museum concise introduction to ancient Rome /
   Nancy H. Ramage and Andrew Ramage.
          p.   cm.
      Includes bibliographical references and index.
      ISBN-13: 978-0-472-03245-7 (pbk. : alk. paper)
      ISBN-10: 0-472-03245-3 (pbk. : alk. paper)
      1. Rome—Civilization. 2. Civilization, Western—Roman influences.
   3. Rome—Antiquities. I. Ramage, Andrew. II. British Museum. III. Title.
   IV. Title: Ancient Rome.

   DG77.R177 2008
   937—dc22   2007041421

Designed and typeset in Minion by John Hawkins
Maps and diagrams by Technical Art Services

HALF TITLE (TOP) A child's sarcophagus, detail. *c.* AD 200.
HALF TITLE (BOTTOM) Coins from the Hoxne hoard. Fourth and fifth centuries AD.
FRONTISPIECE Floor mosaic showing edible fish, *c.* AD 100.
OPPOSITE Statuette of an armed soldier. Bronze. Second century AD.
Photographs © The Trustees of the British Museum

Contents

Preface

This study of Rome and the Romans focuses on the physical remains from archaeological discoveries and collections old and new, allowing a picture of the Roman peoples to emerge and shedding light on their daily lives and culture as well as their politics, law, military might, trade and religious beliefs. One need only look at the front of the British Museum (**opposite below**) to see the influence of the Romans on the architecture of more modern periods. The temple-like façade looks like a Roman temple such as the Pantheon (**opposite above**), and the wings to right and left suggest the colonnades of a Roman public building.

This is not primarily a history book. Rather than studying Roman events in chronological order, we have chosen to introduce specific topics, believing this to be the best way to bring out aspects of the Roman way of life. The rich resources of the British Museum, collected for over 250 years, provide an excellent basis for such a study; they enable the reader to get a good picture of the individual objects that were in everyday use in Roman homes, gardens and public spaces. From coins to chariots, from gods to gladiators, the range is fascinating. The influence of the Romans on later periods is also of great interest, and that, too, is examined throughout the book and discussed in the final two chapters. Quotations are intended to evoke past centuries as well as colourful images of Roman places and monuments in the words of earlier travellers, collectors and scholars.

Andrew Ramage has been studying the Romans since he was a schoolboy excavating at a bomb site in Canterbury and a dig at Verulamium, and for more than forty years at Sardis. Nancy Ramage spent two years at the British School at Rome and also worked for many years at Sardis. More recently, she developed a particular interest in the effect of the Romans on collecting and art in the neoclassical period. Both authors found the teaching of Greek and Roman art and archaeology to be enormously stimulating.

We would warmly like to thank our good friends and colleagues at home, in London and in Cambridge: Fred Ahl, Lucilla Burn, Janet Huskinson, Ian Jenkins, Peter Kuniholm, Richard Mason, Carol Mattusch, Valerie Smallwood, Alexandra Villing, Dyfri Williams and Susan Woodford. Museum records, both on paper and online, have been invaluable. Richard Abdy, Nancy-Jane Rucker and Susan Woodford generously read the text and made valuable suggestions, but should not be held responsible for any errors. We also thank Nina Shandloff at the British Museum Press, and her colleagues Axelle Russo and Beatriz Waters for their help in gathering the illustrations; and especially John Hawkins, both for the design and for his stellar support in the preparation of this work. Finally, we dedicate the book to the memory of George and Ilse Hanfmann, and John and Margaret Ward-Perkins.

Ithaca, New York

OPPOSITE ABOVE The Pantheon, Rome. AD 125–8.
OPPOSITE BELOW View of the front of the British Museum, designed by Sir Robert Smirke. Completed 1847.

Introduction

Any attempt to define who the Romans were is complicated; they may be identified by time period, geography, language or ethnic characteristics, among other features. And any one of these definitions could be applied in a number of different ways. This book concentrates on those aspects of daily life and culture that help to give a picture of the Romans in the largest sense of the word, whether at home or in the public arena, in Rome itself or the wider empire.

1 The Capitoline Wolf. Bronze. Etruscan, *c.* 500 BC. The babies were added in the Renaissance. H. 84 cm (2 ft 9 in).

Rome was founded, according to legend, in 753 BC, and the Romans used to reckon dates from the founding of the city, *ab urbe condita*. The majority of the people who originally lived in Rome were Latins, that is, people who spoke the Latin language, and were related to others in the region called Latium (**fig. 2**). This area was mostly to the south and east of the River Tiber which ran beside the villages that later coalesced to become the city of Rome. The Tiber plays a crucial role in the myth of the founding of the city of Rome, which tells of the twin boys who were abandoned at the river because of a prophecy that they would grow up to kill their uncle. Fortunately, a wolf found and nursed them until a shepherd took over, raising the boys as his own children. Eventually the prophecy came to pass, and Romulus killed his uncle as well as his brother, becoming the founder of Rome. The most celebrated image of this story is the bronze statue of the Capitoline Wolf (**fig. 1**), a splendid animal with milk-filled teats. It is not known if this piece, which is of Etruscan manufacture, actually refers to the story of Romulus and Remus, but it has long been considered to be that mythological wolf. The suckling babies were added during the Renaissance, in the late fifteenth century.[1]

GAULS

Milan

Padua

Venice

Po

Bologna

Marzabotto

Carrara

Rimini

Florence

RUBICON

Arezzo

ETRUSCANS

Populonia

Elba

Tiber

Corsica

Cosa

Tarquinia

SABINES

Rome

CAMPANIANS

SAMNITES

Terracina

Sperlonga

Benevento

Capua

Nola

Melfi

Naples

Mt Vesuvius

Ischia

Capri

Paestum

Brindisi

Sardinia

TYRRHENIAN
SEA

Taranto

ADRIATIC SEA

Inset (top right):

Veii

Cerveteri

Prima Porta

Tivoli

Tiber

Rome

LATINS

Palestrina

Ostia

Alba Longa

Lavinium

0   20 km
0   10 miles

Inset (bottom left):

Naples

Mt Vesuvius

Baia

Herculaneum

Boscoreale

Boscotrecase

Ischia

Pompeii

Sarno

Bay of
Naples

Stabiae

Capri

0   10 km
0   5 miles

Sicily

Agrigento

0   200 km
0   125 miles

N

2 Map of Italy and Latium.

3 Map of the Roman
Empire in the second
century AD.

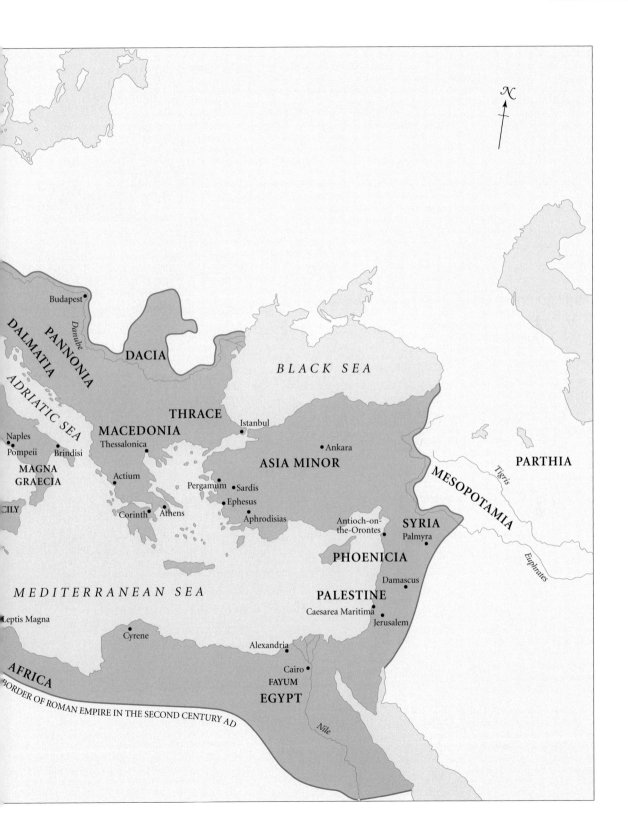

N

Budapest

Danube

DALMATIA

PANNONIA

DACIA

BLACK SEA

ADRIATIC SEA

THRACE

MACEDONIA

Istanbul

Naples

Thessalonica

Pompeii   Brindisi

Ankara

MAGNA
GRAECIA

Actium

ASIA MINOR

PARTHIA

Tigris

MESOPOTAMIA

CILY

Pergamum   Sardis

Corinth   Athens

Ephesus

Aphrodisias

Antioch-on-
the-Orontes

SYRIA

Palmyra

Euphrates

PHOENICIA

MEDITERRANEAN SEA

Damascus

Leptis Magna

PALESTINE

Caesarea Maritima

Jerusalem

Cyrene

Alexandria

AFRICA

BORDER OF ROMAN EMPIRE IN THE SECOND CENTURY AD

Cairo

FAYUM

EGYPT

Nile

11

In fact, from the beginning the Romans had Italic blood, finding their origin in the various tribes that were made up of indigenous peoples who already lived in the peninsula that we know as Italy in prehistoric times. They were people who spoke an Indo-European language, one of those related to a far-flung group ranging from Sanskrit in India to Celtic in northern Europe. Their origins were humble, and in the Iron Age (tenth to eighth centuries BC) it would have been impossible to imagine that a great city, and eventually a great empire, would rise from the scruffy villages perched on the hills above the Tiber in central Italy. Slowly the Roman people became more and more influential within Italy, and eventually dominated those living in the southern part of the peninsula.

A map of the Roman empire in the early second century AD (**fig. 3**) shows the vast areas to which the empire had been extended. The influence of the Latin language, not to speak of Roman law and customs, can be felt to this day in many of the lands brought under Roman rule. Indeed, Roman influence eventually spread far beyond those borders, to the New World and Australia, South Africa, and to the farthest corners of the world.

The Greeks and Etruscans

The people of Rome were under the political domination of the Etruscan kings from the eighth to the sixth centuries BC. These powerful neighbours to the north had amassed great wealth through their rich sources of metal, and through the wide trade that they conducted with the lands to the east. The Etruscans were skilled metal workers who made exquisite works in gold as well as in bronze, ranging from small pins and ornaments to monumental sculpture (such as the wolf just mentioned). Although they lacked a good source of high quality stone, they were masters in working with terracotta (fired clay). In this material they made large-scale sculpture as well as decorated tiles for the exteriors of their temples, and elegant coffins for the wealthiest clients. The Romans, too, at first used a low-grade stone for their buildings and sculpture, but they covered the surfaces of temples with stucco, thus making them white. Centuries later, under the rule of the first Roman emperor, Augustus, the newly opened marble quarries at Luna, near Carrara, provided extensive fine quality white marble for use in architecture and sculpture.

The Etruscans were in close contact with the Greeks as well as with traders who came from Egypt and what is now Turkey, Syria and Israel. In fact this trading network brought about extensive exchanges of goods and ideas that affected not only their material culture but also the religion and politics of the Italian mainland for centuries to come. One of the most important points of contact was in southern Italy, where the Greek city-states had established trading stations and colonies in the eighth and seventh centuries BC. The coastlines of Sicily and the southern part of mainland Italy were dotted with

4 Etruscan helmet.
Bronze. 800–750 BC.
H. 35 cm (13¾ in).

such new footholds from mainland Greece and its islands. Many of these colonies thrived, and some, such as Paestum and Agrigento, still have well-preserved Greek temples that stand as testimony to the grandeur and prosperity of the cities. Through extensive contacts with these newly settled Greeks, the Etruscans found similarites between their own deities and some of the Greek gods, and gave them similar names in their own language. Thus Artemis became Aritimi and Persephone became Phersipnai. Not only were the names taken over, but the visual representation of the gods was quite similar. The forms of Etruscan temples, on the other hand, were quite different from the design used by the Greeks, and it would be Etruscan temples that had a huge influence on those of the Romans (see p. 107).

In the fifth and fourth centuries BC, the classical period in ancient Greek history, art forms and civic government reached new levels of complexity in some parts of Greece, especially in Athens. At this time Rome itself was still a small town with its culture overshadowed by the Greeks, whether in the homeland or the colonies of southern Italy in the area known as Magna Graecia (literally, 'Great Greece'). By the third century, the city was growing and the army was flexing its muscles in Latium, to the south and east. Contact with the Greeks was extensive, partly because many cities in southern Italy and Sicily were taken by force and their inhabitants enslaved. The entire spectrum of Greek classes, from the most to the least educated, was represented among the slaves at Rome. They might become tutors or artisans or menial workers in fields or workshops.

Rome was physically threatened by her much more advanced Etruscan neighbours until the destruction of Veii in the early fourth century BC. They were to have a great influence on the Romans in many ways, including cult practices and building types, like the traditional temple and the round tomb. Nevertheless the Romans did not wish to be part of the Etruscan sphere of influence after they had driven out the last Etruscan king, Tarquinius Superbus, or Tarquin 'The Proud', in 509 BC. After that date, they instituted a republican form of government, in which the balance of powers was a primary principle; the period from 509 to 27 BC is called the Roman Republic. During the later years of this period, the history of the Romans begins to become clearer as events are recorded and archaeological remains fill in the gaps. In 27 BC, a new constitution was inaugurated and Octavian, under the title Augustus, was proclaimed the first emperor (see chapter 1).

Time periods

In the beginning of the Republican period the Romans spent much time battling the cities of the Etruscan League (especially neighbouring Veii) which continually sought to destroy them; and they also were extending their influence among the Latins. Few specifically Roman items have been identified from the early Republican era, and the material culture of Etruscans, Romans and Latins is hard to differentiate. For a detailed account of events, one has to rely on rather biased Roman historians, especially Livy. He belonged to the literary circle patronized by Augustus and wrote descriptions and explanations of the formative years of the Roman people and their character. But the story in this book begins at the point when the Romans have clearly become dominant, when their military might has expanded, and when, through archaeological finds, they become distinct from their neighbours.

During the empire, the reach of the Roman government was extended from Britain to Libya, and from Spain to Syria. Romans had a history of conquering their enemies but allowing them to maintain many of their customs and religions, and in fact the Romans often adopted aspects of the conquered people as their own. It was one of the remarkably successful features of their governing style that they were flexible and willing to absorb foreigners into the system.

Just as difficult as establishing the beginning of the Roman period is the task of determining when the Roman empire ended. The establishment in AD 330 of a new capital, Nova Roma, is sometimes considered the dramatic turning point that signals the end of the old empire and the beginning of a new one. Nova Roma was built on the site of Byzantium, subsequently renamed Constantinople. Another way of determining this point is to mark Constantine's baptism and conversion to Christianity upon his deathbed in the year 337. On the other hand, Roman traditions continued without much change and can be said to have carried on into the sixth century; the inhabitants of Constantinople considered themselves Rhomaioi (Romans), and Latin was in official use for a long time. Some late Roman items in museums are housed in departments largely dedicated to medieval periods, testifying to the difficulty in determining when to stop calling something 'Roman'.

The Romans had a strong sense of history and actively honoured their ancestors. In a tradition called *mos maiorum*, or 'the ways of our forefathers', people looked back on what they considered a golden age of the past. According to Livy, in that golden age, people had a superior sense of morality and a better way of life, and they promoted the rugged individualism that was much admired by later Romans. One of their heroes was Lucius Junius Brutus, who had been instrumental in throwing out Tarquin the Proud, the last Etruscan king of Rome, and instituting the Roman Republic. Brutus' individualism was celebrated in sculpture and coins (**fig. 5**) where his imagined features are made to look handsome and strong. He was also honoured in literature for having had his sons executed for treason and was thus seen as putting the good of the state above that of his family – an important moral lesson for Livy as well as for French revolutionaries about 1800 years later.

The Republic came to a violent end after the death of Julius Caesar in 44 BC, replaced by the empire with the rise of Augustus. The Republic had lasted almost 500 years, and much of the territory later incorporated into the empire had already been conquered during the Republic, but the new form of government would bring greater power to the head of state rather than to the state itself, and a vastly wider influence on the lands around the Mediterranean Sea and beyond. From the late first century BC to about AD 400, or later, Roman emperors ruled with an autocratic hand, even those who were generally benevolent towards the population.

5 Coin, obverse:
L. Junius Brutus. Silver
denarius. c. 55 BC.
Diam. 2 cm (¾ in).

15

Changing attitudes

Just as taste changes in terms of clothing, cars or music, so it changes over time towards historic periods and peoples. Even recently a change has occurred. Until the middle of the last century, few studied Roman art except as an appendage to the Greeks; now hundreds of institutions teach courses on this subject. In the mid-eighteenth century, Johann Winckelmann – secretary to the pope, who was an avid collector of statuary – systematized the study of Greek art and essentially initiated its serious study. But the Romans ranked low in his estimation, and the battle cry for the importance of the Romans was taken up by Giovanni Battista Piranesi (1720–78), a brilliant printmaker who popularized the Roman monuments through his *Views of Rome* (**fig. 6**) and wrote polemical works to defend the Romans against the hellenophiles.[2] Historians and art historians have brought them further into the modern consciousness: *The Decline and Fall of the Roman Empire* by Edward Gibbon (1787), *Roman Art* by Franz Wickhoff (1900) and the many works of Eugenie Strong[3] had a major effect in organizing and bringing Roman accomplishments to the fore. Poets and writers too played a role in spreading interest in the Romans. Nathaniel Hawthorne's *The Marble Faun* (1860) and Thomas Babbington Macaulay's *Lays of Ancient Rome* (1897) were both widely read.

Our view of the Romans has also been shaped by artists and architects who used ancient models and popularized classical taste. At the time of the French Revolution, the early Romans were looked upon as models of morality, and the

6 Giovanni Battista Piranesi, *The Great Baths at Hadrian's Villa.* Etching from the *Views of Rome,* 1770.

painter Jacques-Louis David (1748–1825) portrayed Roman heroes like Brutus as symbols to be emulated by the French people. Nicolas Poussin (1594–1665) before him had also painted Roman historical scenes as examples of virtue. Cultural appropriation of the Romans' art and architecture can be seen in Robert Adam in the eighteenth century, and McKim, Mead and White in the nineteenth and twentieth. Foreign academies in Rome, starting with the French Academy in 1666, further encouraged inspiration from antiquity. The British School at Rome opened its doors in 1901 and the American Academy in Rome, housed in a McKim, Mead and White building, started in 1913.

While travelling to Italy on the Grand Tour was fashionable for those with means in the eighteenth century, it has become extremely popular for the middle classes to travel abroad in our own time. An early twentieth-century guidebook describes the city like this:

> Rome … known even in antiquity as 'the Eternal City', once the metropolis of the ancient world, afterwards that of the spiritual empire of the popes, and since 1871 capital of the kingdom of Italy, is situated in an undulating volcanic plain. … The city proper lies on the left bank of the Tiber, where rise the 'Seven Hills' of ancient Rome. … Deserted for centuries, these have only recently begun to be reoccupied.[4]

The modern city of Rome has become a large urban centre, but always the old, indeed antique, feeling pervades it for anyone who looks around.

In our own time the Romans have come across through cinema, theatre and novels as being a bloodthirsty lot with relatively little culture. A closer look reveals that although there is some truth in this view, they were a much more penetrating and sensitive people than that, making brilliant contributions in the areas of law, government, political theory, architecture, engineering, literature and drama, to name just a few.

From *Ben Hur* and *Spartacus* to *Quo Vadis* and *Gladiator*, films have captivated modern audiences, perhaps partly because they are so gory and wildly dramatic. A BBC television series on the early empire, *I, Claudius* (1976), was based on two novels by Robert Graves, one of the same name and its sequel, *Claudius the God* (1934 and 1935 respectively). Since 2005 another popular television series called *Rome* has appeared. In addition to dramatic presentations relating to Roman characters, several investigations of archaeological puzzles, like the sunshades in the Colosseum or the working of Roman baths, have enjoyed great popularity. One of the most well-regarded books published recently is Robert Harris's *Pompeii* (2003), which describes in vivid detail the destruction of that city, following in the tradition of Edward Bulwer-Lytton's romantic novel *The Last Days of Pompeii* (1834). Overall, the interest in ancient Rome through popular culture is strong and shows no sign of diminishing.

1

City and Citizenship

The original siting of Rome depended on its location by a navigable river, the Tiber, that led to the sea 24 miles (38.6 kilometres) to the southwest. An island in the river made the crossing easier at that point. The low-lying land not far from the river, between the hills nearby, was an area that eventually would become the Roman Forum, or marketplace. This swampy area must have flooded periodically until in the seventh or sixth century BC the farmers built a drain, or *cloaca*, that in a newer construction still carries excess water to the river.

On the east bank, hills afforded protection and places to which the settlers could retreat in time of need. The Romans always claimed that there were seven hills, but which were the actual seven has long been debated (**fig. 7**). The earliest huts were located on the hills, including the Palatine Hill, where traces of post holes and cuttings for flimsy foundations have been discovered. Later, in the first century BC, some of the most prominent politicians and intellects, including the orator Cicero, lived on the Palatine Hill, and eventually some of the emperors built imperial palaces there, hence our word 'palace' from *palatium*, the official name for the hill.

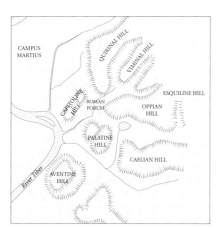

7 Plan of Rome with its hills and the River Tiber.

The highest and most important of all the hills was the Capitoline. Already in the sixth century BC a temple to Jupiter, the most powerful of the gods (see chapter 6), was built on this hill. The fledgling but expanding city, still ruled at that time by Etruscan kings, hired an Etruscan architect, Vulca, to build this huge temple. Its enormous remains, with foundations enclosing a rectangle of 204 x 175 feet (62 x 53 metres), may still be seen within the Capitoline Museum today.

During the Republican period the Romans, needing to defend themselves against threats from the Gauls who were coming from the area of modern-day France, built a defensive wall around the city centre. Erroneously called the 'Servian' wall, after the earlier king Servius Tullius, it was actually built in the fourth century BC (**fig. 8**). As the might of the Roman military grew (see chapter 2), the city itself was less under threat because the battles were fought far away in foreign lands. The city expanded haphazardly as the population flourished and spread along the hills and valleys beside the Tiber. Eventually the area encircled

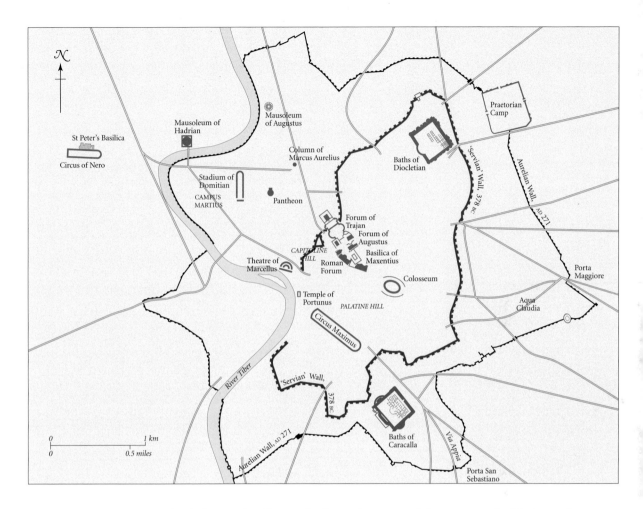

8 Plan of Rome showing the 'Servian' Wall and the Aurelian Wall.

by the 'Servian' Wall proved to be inadequate, and the town stretched far beyond it in all directions. In the third century AD, marauding bands and armies again threatened the interior of the empire, and in AD 271, the emperor Aurelian started to build a huge circuit, the Aurelian Wall, that was finished by Probus ten years later. It was constructed mainly of bricks and concrete as well as fragments of discarded marble taken from other buildings. That wall still stands as testimony to the urgent need to protect the city then, and in subsequent centuries.

In the area of the original huts and the drain that eventually made the area more habitable, a large open area developed into the Forum that remained the core of the city (**fig. 9**). Here the citizens carried out their business; held their markets; built temples and all manner of civic buildings, including the Senate House or *curia*; and had a platform where political speeches were made. A 'sacred way' passed through the Forum, lined on each side by religious and public structures. This large space, with its valuable land in the city centre, was

19

9 The Roman Forum with the Temple of Saturn in the foreground, remains of numerous other temples and streets, and the Colosseum in the far distance.

fortunately preserved for posterity as an open area by a forward-looking archaeologist, Giorgio Boni, in the late nineteenth century. Limited excavations still continue in the area.

One of the Forum's best-preserved temples was dedicated by the emperor Antoninus Pius to his deceased wife Faustina in AD 140; and then, upon his death, the temple was rededicated to him as well (**fig. 10**). This is a splendid example of how Roman buildings often had a second life in later times. The columns across the front and parts of the stairs and the walls of the ancient temple survive because the building was converted into the church of S. Lorenzo in Miranda in the seventh or eighth century, and a distinctive Baroque façade was added at the beginning of the seventeenth century. Many other ancient buildings survive for the same reason, either in whole or in part, in the Roman Forum and elsewhere in Rome. One of the fascinating aspects of the modern city is the countless number of Roman structures that stand in various states of preservation amidst (and under) later buildings.

Citizenship and politics

How the scattered huts of Rome in the eighth century BC developed into the capital of a vast empire is one of the marvels of political history. Through the cunning of its people and a series of successful governmental experiments, a

10 The Temple of Antoninus Pius and Faustina in the Roman Forum. Begun AD 141. The seventeenth-century church of S. Lorenzo in Miranda is built within it.

republican form of government, with two elected consuls at the helm, was established. Military confrontations, ranging from skirmishes to all-out war, played a continual role in determining who would rule Italy and the lands around the Mediterranean; eventually internal crises and civil war brought the republican form of government to an end. Augustus, a great-nephew and adopted son of the dictator Julius Caesar, became *de facto* sole ruler in 31 BC, and the Roman empire was born. From then on, power passed to the next emperor either by family connection or, more often, by orchestrated connivance upon the death of the incumbent.

Roman citizenship changed over time and place, but in general a number of rules applied. A child born to a citizen who had a legal marriage was a citizen. Slaves who were freed, that is freedmen, became citizens, but without the full rights of those who were born citizens. Women were not eligible to vote, although they did have property rights. Soldiers who were active as non-citizen auxiliaries to the Roman army were eligible for citizenship upon their retirement from service. Eventually, in the third century, the emperor Caracalla granted citizenship to all free males within the empire.

Those with citizenship had certain rights that included the right to vote, to make contracts, to marry and have one's children counted as citizens, the right to sue, the right to a trial and the right to hold public office. Citizens could carry their citizenship with them to Roman colonies that were in many cases populated by retired veterans and their families.

The forms of government in Rome had their origins in the early history of the city, going back to the days after the expulsion of the kings when officials served what had been a relatively small population. The organization of the civic administration continued for centuries, and by the time of the later Republic, the administrative functions were greatly extended due to the expansion of Rome from a city to a massive state with a huge population.

Men wishing to secure a place in the government in the Republic and early empire followed a set path in what was called the *cursus honorum*, a political ladder in which politicians were expected to hold public offices with increasing responsibility as they rose through the ranks to attain ever higher political positions. It was also a source of pride to try to reach a position at the earliest age possible for each step. Only aristocrats who were worth a million *sestertii* were eligible to become senators and could climb up this ladder. Each participant was expected to begin his career with ten years of military service, after which he could proceed to higher office.

The first important position along the *cursus honorum*, requiring that the candidate had reached the age of thirty, was that of *quaestor*. At first four men, and in the late Republic twenty men, were elected to this position in Rome, or alternatively someone could serve as *quaestor* under a provincial governor. *Quaestores* looked after the financial affairs of the city and oversaw the importation of grain at Ostia, the port of Rome. The expansion in their numbers shows the need for more and more officials to take care of the ever increasing needs of the state. Julius Caesar increased the number from twenty to forty men.

The next step along the political ladder was the office of *praetor*, an officer who oversaw the army as well as the law courts. Here too the numbers kept increasing, and by the early first century BC eight men held the position simultaneously. The next step on the ladder was to become *consul*, of which there were two at a time, elected for a one-year term. The consuls were in charge of the Senate and served as generals in time of war. Other prestigious positions like that of *censor*, who made up the citizen list, or *aedile*, who looked after city services (especially the public games), also lay along a senator's career path.

The common people, the plebeians, also had a governmental body, an assembly that was led by *tribunes*. By the second century BC, the tribunes who had completed their one-year term could rise to the level of a senator. Because so many of these offices, both of the senatorial and plebeian classes, were for such a short term, a constant flow of inexperienced officials was supported by long-term administrators who knew the ropes and could back them up on the particulars of running the government.

Julius Caesar and the end of the Republic

The Roman Republic faced serious internal problems in the later second century BC when Tiberius and Gaius Gracchus, two brothers usually referred to as the Gracchi, began to foment political and social unrest. They proposed that plebeians, the poor or lower classes, be given land by the state so that they could become farmers; this was to be land that would be confiscated from the patricians, the wealthy landowners. Needless to say, this plan was not well received by the nobles who owned the land, and ultimately they succeeded in blocking the Gracchi's plan. Further unrest and indeed civil war broke out in the early first century BC when two military leaders, Marius and Sulla, fought each other with their armies, each of them in turn committing the unprecedented act of leading their soldiers to Rome and killing many Roman citizens. The Republic never recovered from these violent acts, and the subsequent decades witnessed constant power struggles among the politicians.

A crisis was caused by Julius Caesar, who in 46 BC had been granted dictatorial powers for life. Previously he had been part of a legitimate *triumvirate* (rule by three men) and had then been elected *dictator* several times for a set amount of time, most recently for ten years. 'Dictator' in Roman terms meant that the ruler legitimately had the authority to rule with unlimited power, but this authority had to be renewed periodically by approval of the Senate. Caesar crossed the line when he was declared dictator for life. Those with republican sympathies could not tolerate this, and on 15 March 44 BC he was assassinated.

11 Coin of Julius Caesar. Silver *denarius*. 44 BC, made within the last two months of his life. Diam. 1.9 cm (¾ in), Wt. 3.92 g.

A coin of Caesar crowned with a wreath (**fig. 11**) shows him with long scrawny neck and sharp features. Other portraits, too, show that he had a bulbous cranium, and he was said to have penetrating eyes and a commanding presence. All one need do is read his descriptions of the Gallic Wars – as so many aspiring Latinists still do – to understand what a self-confident personality he had.

The emperors

After Caesar's death, a second triumvirate was formed, consisting of Octavian (Caesar's great nephew, and adopted son), Mark Antony and Marcus Lepidus. Eventually a civil war erupted between the different factions within the triumvirate until Octavian emerged as victor. His final victory, over Mark Antony and Cleopatra VII, queen of Egypt, was at the Battle of Actium in 31 BC. In 27 BC Octavian was proclaimed *Princeps* or First Citizen, a republican title but carrying new meaning. He was given the name Augustus, 'the revered one', which became a title used over and over again by the emperors and even by rulers into early modern times. Other titles that became reserved for the emperor were *Pontifex Maximus*, referring to the emperor's role as chief priest of the Roman gods; and *Imperator*, specifically meaning 'commander'. Many of the traditional imperial titles that are particularly obvious in the repeated formulas on coinage and public monuments derive from names of people or functions from the very beginning; thus, *Caesar* and *Augustus* were titles used by successive emperors. Some emperors went into the field with their troops and gained titular honours for their achievements, such as *Germanicus* for success against the Germans or *Britannicus* after the invasion of Britain.

Augustus was deeply interested in portraits of himself, of which many survive, and in imperial images that reinforced his power.[1] In this he was following the precedent of Julius Caesar, who had put his own image on his

12 Portrait of the emperor Augustus. Bronze, with glass and stone eyes. From Meröe in the Sudan. Probably made in Egypt. *c*. 27–25 BC. H. 47.7 cm (1 ft 6¾ in).

coinage. A large bronze head of Augustus found in Meröe, far up the Nile in the Sudan (**fig. 12**), shows his handsome features with long straight nose, high cheekbones, curvy mouth and strong chin. He also wears the hairstyle characteristic for this emperor, adopted also by other Julio-Claudian emperors, with curved locks falling on his forehead. Also the shape of his head, with bulbous cranium, is found not only in his portraits, but also in those of other family members. This head is unusual because only a few have survived in bronze, and also because the inlaid eyes, made of glass and stone, are still preserved. The jagged edges at the neck indicate that it was torn from a complete statue, probably by a raiding party of Nubians. It was found buried under the steps to a temple of victory, suggesting that by this act the locals were symbolically insulting the Roman emperor.

Another portrait of Augustus (**fig. 13**) appears on a large and magnificent cameo. The stone is brown-and-white sardonyx skilfully carved so that the layers of the variegated stone differentiate the head and shoulders from the background, and give colour to the emperor's cuirass. The details on the armour, similar to that typically worn by the goddess Minerva, show Medusa in the centre surrounded by snakes. The jewelled crown is not ancient.[2] Cameos like this were given as gifts in the closest imperial circles and tended to pass from king to king or emperor to emperor.

Augustus and his wife Livia were married for fifty-two years. She was a strong presence in the imperial family, and for the first time in Roman history, she held real power along with her husband, who bestowed upon her the special title of Livia *Augusta* in his will. Their marriage began in an unconventional and scandalous manner, when both of them divorced their spouses, despite Livia being pregnant at the time with her second child. Nevertheless, on the one hand she promoted marriage and morality and managed to stand in the public eye as a virtuous woman. Her role as the model wife helped to promote the Augustan programme that placed great value on the cohesive family. On the other hand, she was regarded as a scheming woman, determined to ensure that her son Tiberius would ascend to the throne, and a persistent rumour (probably false) suggested that she herself had arranged for Augustus to eat poisoned figs, thus bringing about his death.[3]

Livia was shown in sculpture as rather severe in appearance (**fig. 14**). Her hairstyle was stark, with hair drawn back at the sides and tied in a bun at the back. Over her forehead the strands were brushed up from her face and rounded into a *nodus*, 'wave', and small curls on either side delicately rested on her temples. The empress's hairstyle was imitated by numerous ordinary women of her day, a practice that continued through most of the Roman period.

Livia eventually ensured that Tiberius, her son by her previous marriage,

13 Cameo of the head and bust of Augustus wearing the aegis of Minerva. Sardonyx. H. 12.8 cm, W. 9.3 cm (5 x 3¾ in).

would succeed to the throne. This was after Augustus' two grandsons, Gaius and Lucius, whom he had selected to follow him, both died young. Livia's first husband, of the Claudian family, gave his name to the Julio-Claudian dynasty (the Julius coming from the Julian family of Caesar and Augustus). Tiberius was a rather reclusive fellow and perhaps somewhat bitter for having been previously passed over by Augustus. But he accomplished some public works projects and was generous to cities in Asia Minor that had suffered from a disastrous earthquake in AD 17. After Tiberius came Gaius, better known as Caligula, 'Little Boots' – a nickname given to him when he used to strut around the army camps as a small child. His reign was characterized by fear and loathing for the deranged emperor.

The next ruler was a Claudian too, and in fact his name was Claudius. Claudius was actually Gaius' uncle but his claims on the succession had been overlooked, probably because he was bookish and thought of as not quite competent, due to some physical disabilities. That proved to be an incorrect estimation of his capacity, and he initiated or completed several public works, notably the aqueduct known as the Aqua Claudia near Rome and the harbour at Ostia.

Claudius was fifty years old when he became emperor, and even then was given power more or less by accident. After the death of Caligula, he was hiding in terror as soldiers were rampaging through the imperial buildings, when a soldier saw someone's feet under a curtain. Dragging him out, the soldier recognized Claudius, and proclaimed him emperor. The call was soon taken up by others, and he was declared the next ruler.[4]

Descriptions of Claudius are on the whole not flattering:

He possessed majesty and dignity of appearance, but only when he was standing still or sitting, and especially when he was lying down; for he was tall but not slender, with an attractive face, becoming white hair, and a full neck. But when he walked, his weak knees gave way under him and he had many disagreeable traits both in his lighter moments and when he was engaged in business; his laughter was unseemly and his anger still more disgusting, for he would foam at the mouth and trickle at the nose; he stammered besides and his head was very shaky at all times, but especially when he made the least exertion.[5]

14 Portrait of Livia. Marble. H. 28 cm (11 in).

This report comes from Suetonius, who wrote *The Lives of the Twelve Caesars* in the early decades of the second century AD. He is one of the most important of the ancient sources for giving anecdotes about the first twelve emperors, but his descriptions must be taken with a grain of salt. Roman history is dependent on such sources, although supplemented by information gleaned from inscriptions and archaeology (see chapter 9).

An over life-size bronze portrait of Claudius (or possibly Nero) was found in the River Alde, in Suffolk (**fig. 15**). He is shown with hair combed down on his forehead, somewhat in the manner of Augustus, and with unusually large ears. Claudius was the first emperor to conquer Britain, and it is quite natural that statues of him would be erected in this region. Camulodunum (Colchester), which is not far to the south of the river, had been the capital of the most influential tribe of the defeated Britons, and for a short time became the capital of the Roman province.

The end of the Julio-Claudian dynasty came about upon the death of the emperor Nero in AD 68. He was a wild and depraved ruler, a megalomaniac who arranged for the murder of two wives as well as his mother. He demanded undivided attention and universal admiration when he performed music and sang in public. [6]

BELOW LEFT 15 Portrait of the emperor Claudius, or possibly Nero. Bronze. Found in the River Alde at Rendham, near Saxmundham, Suffolk. First century AD. H. 30 cm (11¾ in).

BELOW RIGHT 16 Portrait of the emperor Vespasian. Marble. AD 70–80. From Carthage. Excavated by Sir Thomas Reade, 1835–6. H. 40.6 cm (1 ft 4 in).

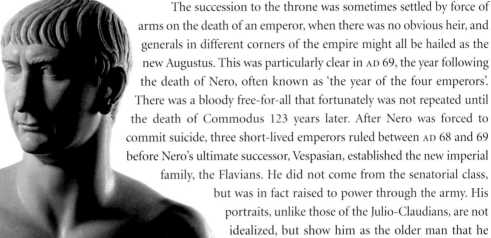

The succession to the throne was sometimes settled by force of arms on the death of an emperor, when there was no obvious heir, and generals in different corners of the empire might all be hailed as the new Augustus. This was particularly clear in AD 69, the year following the death of Nero, often known as 'the year of the four emperors'. There was a bloody free-for-all that fortunately was not repeated until the death of Commodus 123 years later. After Nero was forced to commit suicide, three short-lived emperors ruled between AD 68 and 69 before Nero's ultimate successor, Vespasian, established the new imperial family, the Flavians. He did not come from the senatorial class, but was in fact raised to power through the army. His portraits, unlike those of the Julio-Claudians, are not idealized, but show him as the older man that he was, with features that are both strong and kindly (**fig. 16**). The new emperor was a welcome relief after the wild excesses of Nero. This marble head was excavated in Carthage in the 1830s, at which time it was not felt that it had to be restored; hence the broken nose and ear that were left as found.

When Vespasian was elevated to the throne, he left his son Titus in command of the Roman armies in Palestine, where the Jews had revolted against Roman rule. Titus led a particularly brutal assault against the Jews, and upon defeating them, destroyed the entire great temple in Jerusalem, except one fragment that is called the Western Wall. Upon Titus' return to Rome he was given a triumph, and the Arch of Titus built in his honour records the events on the reliefs (p. 41, fig. 33). After the death of Vespasian, his sons Titus and Domitian ruled in succession; the latter was another of the maniacal types who suspected everyone of being a potential assassin, and set up a system of informers. Domitian built an elaborate palace on the Palatine Hill that was used by succeeding emperors for centuries.

Nerva, the next emperor, ruled for only two years, but his colleague and successor, Trajan, was one of the most important of Roman rulers. He came from Italica, a town in Spain about five miles (eight kilometres) northwest of Seville. He was interested in public works, not only in his native province but across the empire. Trajan was a great military leader, and under his leadership the empire reached its greatest size (p. 10, fig. 3). He also improved the central area of Rome by building a new forum with a large multi-storied market complex attached to it: the Markets of Trajan (p. 76, fig. 65).

A portrait of Trajan (**fig. 17**) shows his typical broad high cheekbones and low bony brow, accentuated by hair that is brushed down over his forehead. His deepset eyes peering out below the brows show a highly intelligent and strong

17 Portrait bust of the emperor Trajan. Marble. AD 108–17. Found near Rome in the Roman Campagna in 1776. H. 67.5 cm (2 ft 3 in).

Bronze statuary

An over life-size bronze head of Hadrian was found in the River Thames near London Bridge in 1834. Hadrian actually visited Britain in about AD 122, travelling far from the capital, and it may have been then that the portrait was made. The beard and moustache are delicately done and the portrait is strikingly handsome.

On the neck of the statue two large square patches can be seen, one of which has fallen out, as well as a number of smaller rectangular patches. These are typical repairs to bronze statuary, used to cover imperfections that occurred during the pouring of molten metal into moulds to produce the hollow-cast bronze. All bronzes above a very small size are hollow so as to reduce the risk of failure and to economize on metal. The holes for patches were cut out around flaws when the surface of the cast bronze was being finished. Then the patches were hammered into place and the surface was polished to a high gleam. If need be, coloured wax could be used to fill any lines that were still visible as well as tiny holes resulting from the formation of air bubbles during casting.

The Romans were skilled metal workers, having learned sophisticated techniques for casting bronze from their Greek, Etruscan and Near Eastern neighbours. Not only did they use these techniques for making sculpture, large and small, but also for vessels, inscriptions and small tools. Larger tools and clamps and nails were made of iron (see p. 77, fig. 66).

18 Portrait of Hadrian, from the River Thames in London. Bronze. Second century AD. Found in 1834. H. 43 cm (1 ft 5 in).

personality. The bust that includes his bare chest shows a new feature that came in under Trajan. On coins he is almost always shown with a wreath on his hair or with rays emanating from his head.

The emperor Hadrian (**fig. 18**) took over after the death of Trajan, his second cousin, in AD 117. Although Trajan was said to have adopted Hadrian in his will, this was never proven, and may have been fabricated by Trajan's wife Plotina. Hadrian was one of the most cultured of Roman rulers and travelled widely throughout the empire. He was smitten by the Greeks, and by Athens in particular, which probably explains why, for the first time among emperors, he wore a beard. He had a wife, Sabina, as well as a beautiful male lover, Antinous, with whom he spent most of his time. When Antinous drowned in the Nile, Hadrian went into deep mourning and then deified the young man.

Hadrian was followed by Antoninus Pius, who started a new dynasty called

the Antonines. It was for him and his wife that the temple in the Roman Forum was built (p. 21, fig. 10). A highly polished over life-size bust of Antoninus Pius wearing a military cloak with woolly fringe was excavated in Cyrene, Libya (**fig. 19**). He was responsible for the construction of the Antonine Wall in Scotland, built to try to extend the empire even farther to the north than Hadrian's Wall.

His successors were two emperors who ruled together from AD 161 to 169: Marcus Aurelius and Lucius Verus (**figs. 20 and 21**). Although they were not actually blood relatives, Marcus Aurelius had been adopted by Antoninus Pius, and Marcus had adopted Lucius Verus in his turn, and gave Lucius his daughter Lucilla in marriage. In their portraits Marcus and Lucius were deliberately made to look alike to confirm the family ties. In fact, Marcus Aurelius was a serious and contemplative ruler and active army general who wrote a collection of essays called *Meditations* in his spare time, while Lucius Verus was characterized in literature as something of a handsome playboy. In the *Description of the Collection of Ancient Marbles*, written by Taylor Combe in 1812, the two are described like this: 'Marcus Aurelius exerted himself unremittingly for the general interest of the Roman people, and was distinguished for the purity of his morals, and the encouragement he gave to learning; while Lucius Verus paid but little attention to the affairs of the state, and passed all his time in indolence,

19 Portrait of Antoninus Pius in fringed military cloak. Marble. *c.* AD 140 or later. From the House of Jason Magnus, Cyrene, Libya. Found by Captain R. Murdoch Smith and Commander E.A. Porcher of the British Navy. H. 71 cm (2 ft 4 in).

RIGHT 20 Portrait of Marcus Aurelius in a fringed cloak. Marble. AD 160–70. From the House of Jason Magnus, Cyrene, Libya. H. 71 cm (2 ft 4 in).

FAR RIGHT 21 Portrait of Lucius Verus wearing a fringed military cloak, tunic and cuirass. Marble. H. with original base 94 cm (3 ft 1 in).

22 Head and bust of the emperor Caracalla. Marble. H. 49.5 cm (1 ft 8 in).

extravagance and debauchery.' The author goes on to say of Lucius, '[He] is said to have been so extremely vain of the beauty of his hair, as to have paid an immoderate degree of attention to it.'[7] Marcus Aurelius' son, Commodus, was one of the rare cases of a natural son taking over the reins of power from his father. But alas, Commodus was yet another of the truly deranged rulers who fancied himself as a god or more often as the hero Hercules, and who brought nothing good to the people.

After Commodus' death there were several competing claimants to the throne; finally a new dynasty began with Septimius Severus, a general who had been commander of the eastern legions. A story that he was related to Marcus Aurelius was probably false, but he encouraged the idea by sporting a long divided beard somewhat reminiscent of that emperor. In fact he came from Leptis Magna, in North Africa – a town that he richly embellished during his reign. His Syrian-born wife, Julia Domna, was a particularly conniving woman who had an evil streak surpassed only by that of her son Caracalla (**fig. 22**).

Caracalla became sole ruler in AD 212 after having arranged to have his brother Geta killed, quite possibly with the collusion of their mother Julia Domna. His brother then suffered *damnatio memoriae*, or the 'obliteration of his memory'. This meant that all references to him, whether in inscriptions or portraits, were destroyed; only a few such instances survive, but often the erasures can be seen. Caracalla had a mean and aggressive face with down-turned mouth and furrowed brow that make clear what a suspicious, not to say vicious, man he was. Typical of portraits of this emperor are his short curly hair, squarish bone structure and sharply turned head with sidelong glance.

Several decades in the mid-third century (AD 235–84) are known as the age of the soldier emperors, a period of great unrest. Emperors came and went as though through a revolving door, and most rose to power through violence, only to be killed soon after by the next ruler. The appearance of all of them is known through their coinage, as each set out to record his face as a way of confirming his legitimacy. Some are known too through brutally realistic portraits. One of the soldier emperors was Aurelian (ruled AD 270–75), the emperor who started the huge wall around the city of Rome before he too was assassinated. On occasion there were several claimants to the throne at one time.

The age of the soldier emperors ended with the accession of Diocletian (ruled 284–305), who was himself the supreme example of the method. He invented a new arrangement of government in which he first divided the empire

23 Medallion of Diocletian.
Gold. AD 284–305.
Diam. 3.9 cm (1½ in).

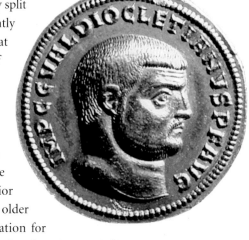

into two halves, west and east, roughly split by the Adriatic Sea, and subsequently divided those areas into two, so that there were four centres of administration. This was called the tetrarchy, which was rule by four emperors at one time. It was arranged so that there were two senior colleagues, 'Augusti', and two junior colleagues, 'Caesares', who were expected to follow into the senior position on the retirement of the older rulers. This produced a radical situation for the emperors in that the office itself, rather than the man holding it, was seen as more important. Uniformity was the watchword, and this is well illustrated in the almost identical portraits on their coins and medals. The magnificent medallion of Diocletian (**fig. 23**) shows him without individualized features, but with the typical square-jawed face, sharp eyebrows, short-cropped hair and stubbly beard of the tetrarchs. The medallion follows the model of Diocletian's coinage but is much larger and heavier, weighing 53.58 grammes, or ten times the weight of a gold *solidus*. The tetrarchic experiment did not last long because of internal suspicion and rivalries that led to civil war in the western half of the empire. The conclusion of the civil war in 312 saw Constantine as the victor, becoming sole ruler in the west.

Roman private portraits

The Romans were clearly great portraitists and left remarkable records of individuals. They learned much about the art of portraiture from their predecessors, the Etruscans, as well as the Hellenistic Greeks, who were already masters at this genre. For instance, the terracotta portrait of a young man (**fig. 24**) from the late Etruscan period, *c.* 300–200 BC, is not an idealized head, but one that shows individuality and character. The slightly over life-size representation shows details such as a mole over the right side of the mouth, large distinctive lips and a sharp line from the left nostril downwards. His hair has a striking pattern of waves and curls. This kind of individuality seems to have inspired the Romans to represent themselves faithfully.

Among the Romans, the practice of carrying likenesses of one's ancestors (*ius imaginis*) was reserved to the patrician class. How the representations were obtained hinges on the physical

24 Etruscan portrait of a
man. Terracotta. 300–200 BC.
Slightly over life-size.
H. 30.5 cm (12 in).

nature of these early likenesses. A metal face mask (p. 140, fig. 146) with few natural features may be part of the tradition. In this case the individual features appear to have been hammered into the bronze sheet from behind in a rather stylized way. The restriction of the *ius imaginis* to the upper class means that the display of these likenesses represents the family's place in society. Thus the commissioning and presentation of the portraits, regardless of the style in fashion at the time, places the sitter and his ancestors high on the societal ladder. Portraits are not confined to tombs: statues of many successful Romans, well before the imperial era, were erected as marks of honour and acknowledgment of important public service.

In the past the tendency has been to identify many Roman statues as copies of Greek prototypes, but now the Romans are given much more credit for their own work. An example of the old school of thought is the British Museum label for the portrait of an old woman with a diadem (**fig. 25**), identified as being 'a copy of a lost bronze original of the early fourth century BC, sometimes identified as Lysimache, a priestess of Athena'. But in fact the piece has distinctly Roman characteristics, especially the descriptive wrinkles on her cheek and jaw.

A good example of the Roman interest in individuality is the portrait head often called 'Pseudo-Seneca', so-named for a Roman philosopher of the first century AD (**fig. 26**), although the actual sitter for this head is not known. The impression given by his aged face, with sagging flesh, sunken eyes and bony

BELOW LEFT 25 Portrait of an old woman. Marble. Found under a pavement in Tarquinia.
H. 25.5 cm (10½ in).

BELOW RIGHT 26 'Pseudo-Seneca'. Marble. One of numerous ancient copies of this head.
H. 32 cm (12½ in).

Personifications

27 Personifications of (left to right) Alexandria, Antioch-on-the-Orontes, Rome and Constantinople. Gilded silver. Found at the foot of the Esquiline Hill in 1793. Second half of the fourth century AD. Rome: H. 14 cm (5½ in).

The Hellenistic period is defined as the period following the death of Alexander the Great in 323 BC up to the victory of Octavian over Mark Antony at the battle of Actium in 31 BC. In this period it became customary to represent a city by a female personification, usually indicated as a walled city by wearing a turreted crown. Romans liked to show the personification of their own city as an armed female figure with helmet and shield, and this goddess, Roma, was often shown with her drapery drawn aside to expose one breast. A set of small hollow-cast silver figures representing four cities includes the personification of Roma, who holds a staff and shield and wears a crested helmet. The others represent, left to right, Alexandria (with cornucopia), Antioch-on-the-Orontes (with turretted crown and an allegorical figure of the River Orontes at her feet) and, after Roma, the turret-crowned Constantinople. These female figures, highlighted with gilding, were found in 1793 at the foot of the Esquiline Hill (one of the seven hills) in Rome. They probably decorated the ends of the handles of a litter or sedan chair that was the standard conveyance for members of the upper classes.

cheeks, is augmented by his scrawny neck and forward-leaning posture. Here is a world-weary but intelligent and sad-looking old man. In Roman painting, too, artists excelled at portraying people in lifelike ways. A small fragment from a larger fresco (**fig. 28**) depicts a man and woman with lively faces, painted with the refreshingly loose brushstrokes that were typical of many painters in the Roman era. Highlights in white and shadows in brown give a sense of volume to the heads, necks and the man's bare shoulder.

28 Fragment of wall painting, head of a man and woman. From Pompeii. Early first century AD. H. 14 cm, W. 17.5 cm (5½ x 6¾ in).

29 Mask of a German with a knot of hair painted yellow, and a moustache and beard. Terracotta. Second century AD. H. 19 cm, W. 17.8 cm (7½ x 7 in).

30 Bust of Africa. Bronze.
H. 22.8 cm (9 in).

Rome and Foreigners

The Romans were an agglomerate of peoples from all over the Mediterranean basin as well as northern Europe, the Middle East and beyond. Because of their interest in accuracy in portraiture, foreigners are sometimes characterized by such details as their hairstyle or dress. A terracotta mask (**fig. 29**) may be identified as a German by the hair that has been tinted yellow and is drawn to the side of the head and tied there in a knot – a feature foreign to Romans in Italy. Although the mask was made in a mould, the craftsman took special care with his tools to embellish the moustache, which again was not a fashion cultivated by the Romans themselves.

A representation of Africa (**fig. 30**) can be seen in the form of a relief plaque with a female bust cast in bronze. She wears a helmet in the form of an elephant's scalp whose trunk has broken off, and only the stump of its right tusk remains. Africa herself supports a small lion at her left side and a tusk from a mature elephant at her right. The whole piece would have been attached by nails

31 Nilotic scene on a relief. Terracotta. First century AD. H. 47.5 cm, W. 60 cm (18¾ x 23½ in).

through three holes in the back. This object might have been part of a set, for the Romans were fond of pictorial representations of particular geographic locations like the provinces or well-known rivers.

Romans sometimes made fun of foreigners or made jokes at their expense; at other times they seemed to enjoy the charm and quaint exoticism of faraway places and their inhabitants. A terracotta plaque showing a Nilotic scene may do both (**fig. 31**). Found in a villa in Rome, it represents two views of the Nile, each bracketed by columns, giving the impression that one is looking at the scene through an arcade. On the left, a crocodile resting on a branch and a barking hippopotamus occupy the river. On the right, a man with caricatured features holds a steering oar and a second man, a naked Pygmy, is rowing their boat. They make their way up the Nile as a crocodile and two ducks lounge nearby. Both scenes have hut shrines (one with a thatched roof) in the background and storks sitting atop the huts and a nearby wall. The scenes may be a parody of Egyptian life, or simply a charming interpretation allowing the viewer to enjoy an exotic foreign place so intriguing to the Romans.

32 One of two bronze plates granting citizenship to Gemellus after twenty-five years of service. 17 July AD 122. From Brigetio, Hungary. H. 16.5 cm, W. 14.8 cm (6½ x 5¾ in).

Two inscribed bronze plates found in Brigetio, Hungary (on the Danube), in ancient Pannonia, record the granting of citizenship to a man called Gemellus (**fig. 32**). He was awarded this honour, after twenty-five years of military service, on 17 July AD 122. Because these plates were found in Pannonia, and because his final term of duty after many other postings was in Britain, he had clearly gone home after being granted an honourable discharge and the concommitant citizenship for himself and his wife. This feature of Roman law, the grant of citizenship to foreigners who served in the military, is one of the ways in which the citizenry continued to grow with a healthy mix of peoples. It was also important for keeping far-flung places from attempting to claim too much independence.

2

The Army at Home and Abroad

In many ways the army was the backbone of the Roman state from the beginning of the Republic, when the body of citizens was not only defending the existence of the fledgling state but also striking out to gain territory. At first the army was composed of small units of farmers who left their fields for a period of time and then returned home for the harvest. The idea of a citizen army was maintained until about 100 BC, when a number of practical reforms were instituted by Marius,[1] who was elected consul several times and became a military hero. What we think of as the standard fighting equipment of a Roman legionary – spears, sword, shield and body armour – dates from this period, as does the introduction of pay and a fixed term of service rather than enlistment for the duration of hostilities. This reorganization was a reaction to several sudden attacks on northern Italy by tribes from Gaul and Germany; it recognized the need for a standing army that would be available to respond immediately rather than being called up and organized anew over a period of weeks or months. The disappearance of a citizen army over time and its replacement by professional soldiers meant that the fundamental idea of defending the homes and public places of Romans and Italians as a duty of citizenship became less central to the purpose of the army, although gaining citizenship remained a prime incentive for many to serve.

Many of the problems of the late Republic (first century BC) and even some responsibility for the government's collapse are due to the requirement that the troops be loyal to their particular commander as the provider of pay and preferment. It was only a short step for armies that were engaged in expanding as well as defending the Roman frontiers to be turned against one another as tools of the ambitious and ruthless politicians in Rome. In fact many of these manoeuvres were carried out by proxy, because the generals were in the field beyond the home *provincia* of Italy, in most cases successfully expanding their control or pacifying rebellious groups. A notable exception to this success was the disastrous defeat of Marcus Crassus in 53 BC by the Parthians at the battle of Carrhae[2] (modern Harran in the far east of Turkey), on the eastern flank of Roman territory. Several legions were lost or captured and their standards (*aquilae*) taken – a signal disgrace to the Roman army, since these were accorded almost sacred status. Eventually, in 20 BC, Augustus was able to retrieve the standards by diplomatic arrangement rather than military engagement – a coup of which he was inordinately proud. Later on, in AD 9, his general P. Quinctilius Varus lost three legions to the Germans in the Teutoburg Forest in Lower Saxony,[3] a disaster that Augustus never forgot.

Organization of troops

A typical legion was composed of about 5.000 heavily armed troops. These were divided into ten groups, 'cohorts', that were nominally made up of about 500 men headed by six centurions. Each of these would be responsible for about eighty-plus men, even though traditionally a century was 100 men. Legionaries, that is the soldiers in a legion, were required to be Roman citizens, but the practice of giving citizenship to retired veterans in the auxiliary units meant that their sons were eligible to serve as legionaries. Within the legion, each heavily armed infantryman carried everything from his fighting equipment to his own pots and pans. The legion was supported by several squads of specialized troops like cavalry or archers, usually drawn from the provinces, and other specialists such as carpenters, doctors and armourers, all required to attend to the needs of this travelling unit. As they marched along, they would build a new camp at each night's stopping place, always following repeatable conventions for a defensive Roman camp, which included soldiers' and officers' tents, a palisade wall and a surrounding ditch. The numbers within the squads changed from time to time but most of the organization dividing larger units into more manageable groups was maintained, as were several of the names for the officers' original functions.

Defence of the frontier was often left to auxiliaries, and the legionaries were kept in reserve. Auxiliaries were made up of non-citizens from within the empire, and of soldiers who had been conquered and were subservient to the Roman government. The differences were mostly in status and pay. The organization of auxiliary units was much like that of the legions, but there tended to be more of them. In the second century AD about two-thirds of the Roman army was made up of auxiliaries.

The organization of the army was based on the classes into which the citizenry was divided. For the senatorial class, a successful career in public life was predicated on advancement through several junior military positions before one could be considered ready for the heavier responsibilities of managing a province and commanding the troops that went with it. Such men were considered to be experienced because of their military training and thus were prepared to become senators and administrators. Lower classes performed lower-ranked duties within the army, of which the centurion was one of the most important. The auxiliaries (like Gemellus, p. 37, fig. 32), who were not originally Roman citizens, also played an important supporting role in the success of the army.

In practice the units were not always up to strength, judging from a tablet from Vindolanda in the North of England that described the staffing status of an auxiliary unit, the First Cohort of Tungrians.[4] It lists the details of attendance, showing that it was understaffed:[5]

Vindolanda Tablet II.154

18 May, net number of the First Cohort of Tungrians, of which the commander is Iulius Verecundus the prefect, 752, including 6 centurions.

Of whom there are absent guards of the governor at the office of Ferox		46
at Coria including (?) 2 centurions		337
at London (?) a centurion		
… outside the province including 1 centurion		6
set out (?) to Gaul including 1 centurion		9
at Eburacum (?) [York] to collect pay		11
at (?)		(?) 1
[No readable explanation for absence]	45	
total absentees including 5 centurions	456	
remainder, present including 1 centurion		296
from these:		
sick		15
wounded		6
suffering from inflammation of the eyes		10
total of these		31
remainder, fit for active service including 1 centurion	265	

Thus, to summarize: for a cohort that should have had 500 men on active duty, only 265 were available for service. The others were sick or absent for one reason or another.

The triumph

Naturally enough, the material record concentrates on the successes of the Roman army. Triumphal monuments and smaller decorative items would be bestowed upon a victorious general. If he had soundly defeated the enemy and killed or taken prisoner a sufficient number of troops and carried off a large quantity of booty, he could be voted a 'triumph' by the Senate. A precise procedure was followed that required the general to remain with his troops beyond the city limits until the vote was certified. A procession was then formed consisting of the senators, important prisoners in chains and the booty, along with placards and paintings of the campaign. The *triumphator* would ride in an elaborately decorated chariot that was designed especially for these occasions, and the army would follow. During the empire, the emperor alone took all the glory for his generals' triumphs.

Triumphal arches were built for various emperors for such events. The Arch of Titus (**fig. 33**) is one of the best preserved in Rome, although it had to be re-erected and restored in modern times.[6] It was constructed for Titus after his

33 The Arch of Titus, Rome. *c.* AD 81. H. *c.* 15.5 m (50 ft).

death, to commemorate his victory over the Jews in Jerusalem. The Jews had revolted against Roman rule in AD 66, leading to the Jewish war that finally ended in AD 72 with the fall of Masada. The triumphal arch was built at one end of the Roman Forum on the Via Sacra. A relief at the crown of the vault showing Titus being carried skyward on an eagle, an image of his apotheosis, is part of the interior decoration. The two main reliefs under the arch both represent sections of the triumphal procession: one shows the emperor in his chariot along with soldiers and allegorical figures, and the other the soldiers marching with placards announcing their successes. Part of the booty they snatched from Jerusalem when they defeated the Jews under Titus was the great gold menorah from the Temple. This is prominently displayed on the relief under Titus' arch.

The procession entered the city by the Porta Triumphalis and followed a circuitous route up to the Temple of Jupiter on the Capitoline Hill, where a sacrifice was held. The sacrifice that was performed to commemorate a triumph may be reflected in a terracotta architectural relief showing the slaying of a bull (**fig. 34**). The naked woman, an allegorical representation of Victory, has large wings with articulated feathers and drapery flowing behind her. She dramatically holds back the bull's neck and wields the knife in her right hand. A sacrificial incense burner or candelabrum stands at the right.

34 Architectural relief with Victory sacrificing a bull. Terracotta. Late first century BC or early first century AD. H. 23 cm, W. 38 cm (9 x 15 in).

THE ARMY AT HOME AND ABROAD

35 Relief panel with triumphal procession.
Terracotta. First–second century AD.
H. 33 cm, W. 38 cm (13 x 15 in).

36 Captive barbarian.
Marble. Late first century AD.
H. 86 cm (2 ft 10 in).

A terracotta panel (**fig. 35**) represents a triumph where a heavy cart carries two barbarian prisoners being tormented by their captors and showing clear signs of suffering in their expressive faces. Careful details in the terracotta relief include the chains that are attached to their ankles and torques (heavy metal bands around their necks), and knobs on the side of the cart. Their torques and baggy trousers identify them as barbarians; they may well be Dacians taken prisoner by the emperor Trajan. A marble statue of a captive barbarian, kneeling and with hands tied behind his back, also wears the signature baggy trousers as well as the Phrygian cap often worn by captives (**fig. 36**). His long hair, too, identifies him as a foreigner, and his open mouth and expressive upturned face indicate that he is begging for mercy. The drapery of a second figure who must have been standing over him is also preserved. This statue was found in the so-called 'Palace of Trajan' at Ramleh, near Alexandria, where a legionary fort once stood.

43

Army equipment

Soldiers were armed with heavy protective gear that was usually made out of bronze, but sometimes iron. A bronze statuette of a fully armed soldier (**fig. 37**) shows how such a figure would look. He wears a crested helmet with chin strap, a short tunic with fringed flaps, a cuirass, leg protectors and sandals – though often soldiers wore boots instead. This statuette is bearded and his eyes are inlaid. Army gear often depended upon which unit one was in. For instance, a Roman legionary soldier would probably have worn chain mail in the early empire, or he might have worn segmented plate armour, that is, rectangular pieces of bronze riveted or strapped together, making a better protective suit.

Sometimes men in the military participated in sports events, in which case they would wear special equipment for the occasion. One such piece is the bronze cavalry sports helmet from Ribchester (**figs. 38 and 39**), found in 1796.[7] The front is in the form of a beautiful male face, with slits at the eyes for the wearer to peer through and additional holes at the mouth and nostrils. On the helmet itself, cavalry and infantry scenes in shallow relief decorate the crown of the head, while below the protective flange, on a diadem over the front of the hair, are mythical figures, including a snaky-legged god. Two snakes slither down on to the side of the mask's cheek above a chin strip that holds the diadem in place. The face is separate from the helmet at the back, but the two would have been attached with leather straps. The helmet would have been worn in cavalry shows where elite units performed for the troops and conducted mock battles.

The material record of the army's gear is quite uneven because of the vagaries of survival and preservation. As with household goods, the more elaborate were given more care and attention.

A remarkable sword, called 'The Fulham Sword', was found at Fulham, London, in the River Thames (**fig. 40**). An iron blade was housed in a bronze sheath, the main part of which is richly decorated with the tendrils of an acanthus plant and two birds that drink out of the calyx of the flower. At the top of the sheath is the image most associated with the founding of Rome: Romulus and Remus being suckled by a she-wolf (see p. 8, fig. 1).

37 Statuette of a fully armed soldier. Bronze. Second century AD. H. 10 cm (4 in).

38 Cavalry sports helmet. Bronze. From Ribchester, Lancashire. Discovered in 1796 by a clogmaker's son. Late first or early second century AD. H. 27 cm (11 in).

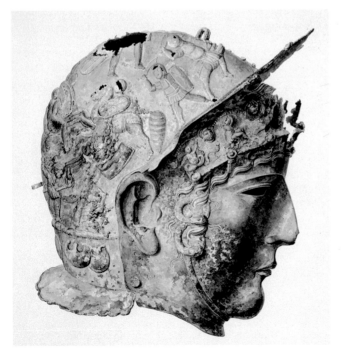

39 The Ribchester Helmet in profile, in a watercolour attributed to Thomas Underwood, 1798.

40 The Fulham Sword. Iron blade and bronze sheath. Found in the River Thames at Fulham, London. First century AD. L. 56 cm (22 in).

45

Crocodile parade suit

A soldier's special mock-armour made from the skin of a crocodile would have been worn as a parade suit. The larger scales from the back of the crocodile skin are on the front of the suit, and smaller scales, more suitable for movement, are used to cover the soldier's legs. The suit consists of body armour and a helmet. Radiocarbon dating has placed it in the third century AD.

Roman soldiers stationed in Egypt participated in local customs and were particularly intrigued by the cult of crocodiles, a ubiquitous creature on the Nile. The crocodile, thought to be a sacred beast, embodied Sobek, the crocodile god. The Roman geographer Strabo (17. 8.11) reported in the first century BC that he and the Roman governor of Egypt went to a sacred lake where lived a tame crocodile, a representative of the god Sobek. The belief was that if a visitor to the pool called the god and Sobek turned towards him, then the god would be fed meat, a biscuit and wine, and this was a good omen. If the crocodile did not respond, that was a bad sign.

When the crocodile who embodied Sobek died, he was mummified, and a new crocodile was found to replace him. The numerous mummified crocodiles found in Egypt are testimony to the widespread cult. The crocodile also served as assistant to the gods on numerous occasions, most notably in helping Isis to recover the dismembered parts of her brother and consort Osiris, as well as the lost hand of the god Horus.

41 Crocodile parade suit. Made of crocodile skin. Third century AD. Found in a grotto in Manfalout (ancient Lycopolite), Egypt. H. 49 cm (19.3 in).

The personal side of the army

Tombstones and memorials bring the reader close to the personal stories of individuals from the past, and sometimes the inscriptions can be quite touching. A soldier named Ares (appropriately enough, as Ares was the Greek god of war) is commemorated by a marble memorial or tombstone that represents him twice (**fig. 42**). The young man died at the age of twenty-nine, probably between AD 160 and 180. On the left the figure is seen as a soldier wearing a military cloak (*paludamentum*) and a tunic. He may hold a scroll in his right hand, above a sacrificial flame. If it is a scroll, it may represent his discharge papers. On the right he stands again, now in civic dress, namely the toga. His helmet, shield and sword are beside him. The inscription, in Greek, reads as follows:

> His military service completed, Ares dedicated his weapons and his period of service to Ares. Having left these things, he was taken to a world without order, where nothing but darkness exists.[8]

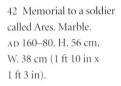

42 Memorial to a soldier called Ares. Marble. AD 160–80. H. 56 cm, W. 38 cm (1 ft 10 in x 1 ft 3 in).

Soldiers serving tours of duty in distant lands must have become quite homesick and would have longed for the pleasures of home. A remarkable series of wooden tablets with written texts have been discovered since 1973 at successive forts in Vindolanda, northern England, shedding invaluable light on the life of soldiers before the building of Hadrian's Wall. The Vindolanda forts were occupied between about AD 85 and 120. Although fragmentary, the texts reveal all kinds of interesting information, such as requests from soldiers for foods that they couldn't possibly get in the north of England, which must have reminded them of home. Examples are requests for olives and pepper, and a letter saying that someone has sent a soldier fifty oysters.[9] One complains in a letter, 'My fellow-soldiers have no beer. Please order some to be sent.'[10] Others record such mundane things as shopping lists, an invitation to a birthday party[11] (**fig. 43**) and inventories of items, probably to be used in the camps. Another reports sending socks, sandals and two pairs of underwear to someone else.[12] One seems to be a recipe found in the commandant's wife's kitchen.[13]

When a soldier was ready to leave the army, he needed to have his 'papers' in writing. Trajan issued a bronze military diploma (**fig. 44**) to a Spanish junior officer, Reburrus, in AD 103. The word 'diploma' means, literally, 'something folded' or 'double' and refers to a two-leaved document. Reburrus' diploma granted him citizenship and the right to legal marriage, a right normally awarded to auxiliary soldiers upon their retirement from service.[14] Official records such as this, like their gravestones and letters, help to provide insight into the personal lives of soldiers. Because they include details of postings, they also help us to understand the make-up and movement of the units of the army around the empire.

43 One of the Vindolanda tablets: a birthday invitation from Claudia Severa to Sulpicia Lepidina. From Vindolanda. Wood. H. 9.6 cm, W. 22 cm (3½ x 8½ in). Vindolanda Tablet II.291.

44 The two leaves of the
military diploma of
Reburrus. Bronze. AD 103.
H. 16.5 cm (6¼ in).

45 View of Hadrian's Wall.
L. 117 km (73½ miles).

The emperors and defensive walls in Britain

The soldiers at Vindolanda were protecting the northern flank of the Roman empire. Julius Caesar twice attacked Britain, in 55 and 54 BC, while fighting the Gallic wars, but had not successfully taken territory in Britain for the Roman state. The emperor Claudius first conquered the Britons in AD 43, and subsequent emperors maintained and expanded Rome's control of the island. But it was Hadrian who built the substantial wall that still stands across northern England (**fig. 45**). This remarkable undertaking made a barrier across the narrowest point of Britain (73½ miles; 117 kilometres)[15] from coast to coast. The wall ranged from a width of 6 to 10 feet and was about 15 feet high (W. *c.* 2 to 3 m; H. *c.* 5 m). A V-shaped ditch, or *vallum*, was dug in front of it. Its interior of rubble was faced with cut stones joined with mortar. The wall was augmented by mile forts, with two turrets between each mile, and larger garrison forts every few miles.[16] In addition, the wall follows a ridge for much of the distance, thus adding both to its protective capacity and to the view afforded across the landscape to the north.

Some years after Hadrian, in AD 142, Antoninus Pius ordered that yet another wall be built further to the north, in Scotland. It was constructed with earthworks rather than with stones and had a deep and wide ditch built at its base. Despite these efforts, it did not hold back the enemy for long, and in AD 181 Roman soldiers were forced to retreat south to Hadrian's Wall, which stood as the northern boundary until around AD 410. At that time the Romans officially left Britain for good, although their influence never completely disappeared.

3

Industry, Agriculture and Communications

The Romans developed remarkable skills in administration and engineering. Many tangible signs remain to this day, and the size and enduring nature of their constructions are testimony to their ability to build roads, aqueducts, bridges and ports, as well as to their expertise in devising mechanical devices for industry and agriculture. Their success in these areas meant, first, that Romans, in particular the army, could get from one place to another along well-marked roads that were frequently paved with large, long-lasting blocks, and drained towards the gutters at the roadsides. Bridges spanned wide and deep valleys, and aqueducts brought fresh water in abundance from springs and reservoirs to cities and towns, enabling the people to have fountains, public baths, toilets and other water-dependent amenities. The construction of artificial harbours improved conditions for seafarers, particularly merchants.

Roads

Roman roads were originally arteries for the army, linking Rome's territories, connecting colonies, and helping to pacify previously hostile areas. On the other hand, roads had been laid and even cut through rock under the Romans' predecessors, the Etruscans, and sometimes Roman roads followed Etruscan paving in urban areas. The Persians before them had made roads that covered great distances and led from their cities in western Asia Minor, including Ephesus and Sardis, to their capitals in the east: Susa, Persepolis and Ecbatana. But Persian roads were mostly tracks that followed the easiest routes through the land. Although the Hellenistic Greeks paved some of their streets,[1] no other ancient peoples constructed such an elaborate and widespread trunk road system as the Romans. In fact, it was their roads that enabled them to reach the distant regions of what would become a vast empire.

In many cases, Roman roads are the basis for roads that still exist today – in England, on the European continent, and in North Africa and the Middle East. The many straight roads that lead from one place to another are often set on top of older Roman roads. In some places the actual paving stones of the Roman road still exist, such as on some parts of the ancient Via Appia that lead

Paving blocks

On the whole, the paving blocks on roads lasted extraordinarily well over the centuries, but they became rutted by wheels that repeatedly went over the same tracks. In Pompeii, the ruts went quite deep where the wheels of carts had to be driven between the stepping-stones. These stones were placed at intervals, especially at crossroads, to allow pedestrians to cross the street without getting their feet wet or covered in dung, and they forced wheeled traffic to follow more or less the same track every time. Urban streets had high kerbs that tended to keep rainwater in the roadway until it could empty into the drains that ran under the middle of the streets. City drains were covered with flat, rectangular paving stones, a practice in contrast to country roads, where drainage was effected by setting the crown of the road higher than the edges. This practice, known as cambering, is still in use today.

46 Street showing stepping stones and ruts: the Via degli Augustales, Pompeii.

47 Milestone. AD 120–21. From Llanfairfechan, Gwynedd, Wales. H. 1.67 m (5 ft 5¾ in).

OPPOSITE 48 Construction of a Roman road with basalt blocks. Etching by Giovanni Battista Piranesi, from the *Antichità Romane*, 1756.

from the south side of Rome itself; stretches of this road were still in general use until the late nineteenth century. Streets that have been excavated at Ostia Antica, Herculaneum and Pompeii, as well as other cities, still have paving stones in place.

The Romans were masters at marking their roads and recording distances. Milestones, called *miliaria* in Latin, come from the word *mille*, 1000, for the 1000 paces that make up a Roman mile. They are usually round and about 6 feet (2 metres) or higher and set on a square base. The stone is granite, limestone, sandstone or basalt, or whatever the best local quarries could provide. One found in Wales near the fort of Canovium (Caerhun) was erected under Hadrian, in about AD 122, and was placed 8000 paces (7 modern miles, 11 kilometres) west of the camp (**fig. 47**). The inscription was probably highlighted in red paint. In addition to recording the distance, the official titles of the emperor in power were added, and sometimes the name of the provincial governor as well. Such markers could be found not only near cities and forts, but also in deserts and wild mountain passes. They usually marked the distance to (or from) a fixed point such as a gate or a mark in the nearest town centre.

Milestones also served to record repairs to the roads. One set up in Spain in AD 79 tells that the emperor Vespasian had 'restored the Augustan road from the Arch of Augustus to the Ocean, built bridges, and restored the old ones'.[2] The markers too would sometimes be updated, with additional restorations added as appropriate. Later still, a Roman milestone would often be adorned with a cross near the top; and sometimes a Christian roadside shrine would be set up beside it, as the ancient marker seems to have been a venerated spot long after its pagan sponsors had gone.

The eighteenth-century artist Piranesi was fascinated by the ways in which the Romans constructed everything from pavements to monumental buildings, and he made etchings of the buildings themselves, and of such technical details as the paving stones and foundations of roads (**fig. 48**). The stone surfaces are typically made from tightly fitted, naturally faceted blocks of volcanic basalt, where available, that are set over several layers of bedding material composed of small stones.

The streets in much of Rome itself were narrow and twisted, and the high buildings both shut out the sunlight and caused the sounds of wheeled traffic on the pavement to reverberate with deafening noise. Carts were banned during the day, but this made the nights horridly noisy. Juvenal described the situation:

Insomnia causes more deaths amongst Roman invalids than any other factor. … How much sleep, I ask you, can one get in lodgings here? … The waggons [thunder] past through those narrow twisting streets, the oaths of draymen caught in a traffic-jam . …[3]

49 The gorge where Via Mala, a treacherous Roman road, passes through. Graubunden, Switzerland. Also seen are two bridges, one eighteenth- and one nineteenth-century, and a twentieth-century avalanche protector.

50 Roman column at the summit of the Julier Pass. Graubunden, Switzerland.

Roman roads in the countryside went in straight lines where this was possible, but they followed the lie of the land when required. When passing through the mountains and valleys of the Alps, in what is now Switzerland, the incredible skills of their engineers were called upon, and treacherous tracks that hug steep canyons can still be used today. One of these tracks, called the Via Mala, passes near Chur (ancient Curia) from Thusis to Zillis, in the canton of Graubunden, and joins further roadways towards Italy through the San Bernardino Pass. A narrow and difficult track was cut in the rock just above a precipitous drop that falls into the swirling river below (**fig. 49**). The dramatic and beautiful gorge is 500 metres high.

Today the Julier Pass climbs to a great height in order to get from modern Tiefencastel to St Moritz. The Romans built a small temple at the summit as a place where travellers could give thanks for having accomplished the steep and daunting climb. Two of the columns from that temple, still marking the highest point, are a reminder of the antiquity of this ancient roadway (**fig. 50**). Local inhabitants of this region of Switzerland, the canton of Graubunden, still speak an ancient language, Romansch, that goes back to a dialect from Roman times.

Many of the ancient place-names that have become the names of modern towns can be recognized on the so-called Peutinger Table, a late Roman map that was copied by a monk in the thirteenth century. It was recognized for what it was in the late fifteenth century and given to Konrad Peutinger, after whom it is named. Originally twelve long and narrow sheets of parchment (one of which is missing) put together horizontally for a length of 21 feet (6 metres) gave a distorted but fascinating view of the ancient world. Not only are the towns labelled, but the distance between them, in Roman miles, is given in Roman numerals. Curia is identified, and the Via Mala may be indicated but is not labelled. Three great cities of the later Roman empire, Rome, Constantinople and Antioch, are singled out on the map with allegorical images, not unlike those representing cities in silver (see p. 33, fig. 27), and many other cities and towns as well as rivers, forests, roads and even hostels are shown.

Pipes

Lead or clay pipes brought clean water into some wealthy private houses and public baths and fountains, and dirty water fed into the street drains where it was carried away. The pipes were made of segments, wider at one end than the other, that were inserted into each other, making them easy both to lay and to repair (**fig. 51**).[4]

Whereas manmade channels and pipes of lead and terracotta were used in Italy, other methods were preferred elsewhere in the empire. For instance, in Britain wooden pipes were often used, and in the east, walls within wadis, or gullies, were the method of choice. This allowed for the channelling of the

51 A pile of pipes,
Ephesus, Turkey.

infrequent rainwater, for example in Palestine, which was conquered by the
Roman emperor Titus in the first century AD. Eventually the Romans adopted
the local methods of the area. Gullies that were usually dry became important
water sources during rainfall, and the water that was captured was reserved for
times of need. This method made it possible to supply sufficient water in the
third century to the cities of Sabratha and Leptis Magna in modern-day Libya.[5]

Arches, bridges and aqueducts

Aqueducts are among the most spectacular examples of Roman engineering.
Frontinus, commissioner of the aqueducts under Trajan, wrote a definitive book
about them, in which he asked, with pride, 'Will anybody compare the idle
Pyramids, or those other useless though much renowned works of the Greeks
with these aqueducts, with these many indispensable structures?' [6]

The Romans had the benefit of some basic preparations from the Etruscans:
'The Etruscans … had but an elementary knowledge in general of the science of

hydraulic engineering. Owing to the natural conditions of their land, however, they became familiar, at a very early time, with the use and construction of underground drains and sewers of a simple type, as is clear from the existing remains.'[7] Eventually, the Romans determined that they could expand the underground channels into elevated aqueducts that carried water long distances supported by arches, in the manner of earlier sewers and drains that had been beneath the surface.

In Rome, the first formal water commissioner (*curator aquarum*) was Agrippa, son-in-law of Augustus. Under his patronage a new aqueduct, the Aqua Julia (named for Augustus' family line) was constructed across the Roman Campagna. 'For the better distribution of the water of the various conduits, a large number of new local reservoirs and fountains was built in the different regions, comprising seven hundred basins, five hundred fountains, and one hundred and thirty reservoirs.'[8] All of these were needed to provide an adequate water supply to the city of Rome that had grown so rapidly.

After the death of Agrippa in 12 BC, Augustus himself took on the responsibility for the aqueducts; and as many of those already built had technical problems and leakages, he undertook the repairs on a grand scale, at his own expense. Two new laws passed by the Senate required property owners to supply building materials at a fair price, and claimed the right to remove trees or other debris from the line of the aqueduct. Augustus set up markers, rather like milestones, to record the repairs along the route.[9] This was to ensure that he got credit for the work which, by extension, would bring glory to the imperial house.

Water was brought to the cities by many miles of aqueducts that led from a source such as a spring or clear stream in the hills nearby. Most familiar are the great arcaded constructions that the Romans used to bridge deep valleys. This is particularly obvious in the enormously long parade of arches bringing the water of the Aqua Claudia into Rome across the plain of the Campagna. But many miles of the system were composed of underground channels and wide clay pipes, and occasionally narrower lead ones, depending on the quantity of water required. These constructions were needed to supply towns that typically could not provide enough water from their own local sources for a large urban population.

In southern France, the Pont du Gard aqueduct (**fig. 52**) still stands, having formerly carried water across the valley of the Gardon River to the city of Nemausus (modern Nîmes). The structure, with three levels of arches, covered only a small portion of the 30-mile (48.3-km) conduit, which had a continuous downward slope for its entire length. The rest was a channel that was mostly underground. The aqueducts relied upon gravity for the water to flow down to its ultimate destination. The gradient had to be steep enough to keep the water flowing but gentle enough to prevent too much pressure from building up.

52 The Pont du Gard,
Nimes. Mid-first
century AD. Sandstone.
H. 49.38 m (162 ft).

The main purpose of the aqueducts was to bring clean water into public baths and fountains; provision of water to private houses was a secondary benefit and required specific permission. The water ran continuously like a series of small streams through the basins and latrines until it was fed into the main street drains or *cloacae*, where it was carried away. Unauthorized tapping into the public system was a criminal offence and subject to a heavy fine.

Roman aqueducts, scattered all across the Roman empire, are frequently best preserved in remote areas with low population density, but there are some striking urban examples that continued to serve as water sources for a long time. Those around the city of Rome are perhaps the best known, not only because of their actual preservation and visibility but also because their qualities and capacities were described in the text by Sextus Julius Frontinus. He was a successful Roman administrator who had been appointed *curator aquarum* by the emperor Nerva, and he continued in this role under Trajan. There were nine aqueducts in Rome by the time of his death in AD 104, only one of which, the Aqua Traiana, had been built under his care; three more were to be built later, all supplying the city of Rome.

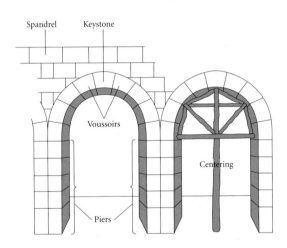

53 Drawing of an arch
showing weight
distribution.

Bridges too were usually supported by arches, and many of these strong and durable constructions have survived to our own day. One example, the bridge of Alcantara in central Spain (**fig. 54**), is still in use for vehicles and pedestrians and is the only road across the Tagus River for about 100 miles (160 kilometres), either to the north or south. It was built in AD 105 under the emperor Trajan, as we know from an inscription on the arch that spans the roadway in the centre of the bridge. Its continuing importance is implied from its very name, simply 'The Bridge' in Arabic.

The Romans were not the first to use the arch (the Greeks and Etruscans already knew about the form), but they were the first to capitalize on its potential. A stone arch is made up of square blocks placed one on top of another to make the vertical supports; voussoirs, or wedge-shaped blocks, are then placed in an arc on top of the verticals (**fig. 53**). The central voussoir, called the keystone, is the final piece that locks the stones of the arch together, and from which the weight of the superstructure is transferred, through all the other blocks, outwards and downwards on to the vertical supports. Arches are strong, with the added advantage that they require relatively little material (compared, for instance, to a solid wall); furthermore, in stormy weather, the wind goes through the arch without endangering the stability of the structure. This can be a huge asset when

54 The bridge at
Alcantara, Spain. Granite.
AD 105. L. 204 m (670 ft).

used on a massive scale in bridges and aqueducts that span rivers or valleys.

A sort of scaffolding, called 'centering', is first constructed in wood in the shape of the arch, and the voussoirs rest on it until the keystone has been inserted. At that point the arch will stand on its own, and the centering is removed. In a series of arches, such as on an aqueduct or bridge, the wood of the scaffolding is used again for each successive arch. The process is efficient and economical and the result both strong and aesthetically pleasing.

Ports and harbours

As the Romans needed more food and goods to supply their growing population, they embarked on a major effort to increase their commercial suppliers overseas. This meant pursuing a maritime trade of unprecedented proportions, reaching from Spain to North Africa and Egypt. Many of the coastal cities that the Romans came to control already had good harbours; a favourable location on a well-protected bay must have been one of the original reasons for choosing the site. As trade built up, however, the need for additional facilities necessitated extensions for the moorings as well as new warehouse storage at those places where Roman commerce was concentrated.

The Romans were also able to build artificial protection enabling ships to moor and unload in what would otherwise be inhospitable locations. They altered and expanded existing buildings and improved access for much bigger and bulkier loads, including the monolithic columns that their architects increasingly favoured. The invention of concrete as a building material can be seen as the key to this bold challenge to the laws of nature. Several ancient authors marvelled (or complained) about the builders around the Bay of Naples, who pushed great masses of concrete into the sea in order to make piers and jetties, some of which can still be seen below the water along the coastline, especially at the bay at Baia. The sea has since risen to cover what had previously projected above the water line.

The fish feel the sea getting smaller for the masses being dumped into the sea.

Horace, *Odes* 3.1

Still surviving is the port of Caesarea Maritima in Israel, built between 22 and 9 BC by Herod the Great, a local ruler in the kingdom of Judaea who held on to power with the approval of the Roman government. A large basin was recently explored, exposing the great jetty built out into the sea where no existing headland or offshore island had offered protection. This stretch of coastline is more or less flat and subject to storms and surf from the west.

The port constructed by the emperor Claudius near Ostia, which had long been the port of Rome, was placed at a natural outlet where the River Tiber emptied out into the Mediterranean Sea. In fact, the word *os* in Latin means 'mouth'; hence *Ostia* is the mouth of the Tiber. As Rome's power grew and fleets of boats were bringing in grain from Sicily and Egypt, the original harbour of Ostia proved inadequate. Under Claudius, a huge undertaking was begun, against the advice of his architects: a new port was dug about two miles (3.2 kilometres) north of the old one.[10] There he built a large jetty near the mouth of the Tiber for the protection of the ships. This became known as *Portus*, meaning 'harbour' (see p. 75). Much of the success of the material, first used about 200 BC, rested on the fact that Roman concrete would set underwater, thanks to a chemical reaction rather than just a drying process.

The excavations at the city of Ostia have revealed evidence in the form of floor mosaics for a network of traders moving goods and people. These mosaics advertised the activities and headquarters of several of the traders around the Mediterranean. They were set within a colonnade in a large rectangular complex, today called the Piazzale delle Corporazioni (Square of the Guilds), with offices and shops near the ancient theatre. The offices of the particular

55 Mosaic of a lighthouse. Piazzale delle Corporazioni, Ostia.

traders were set behind the descriptive mosaics. One of these depicts a lighthouse that was certainly the one at Ostia (**fig. 55**). It has flames shooting out of the top, while boats ply the harbour at its base. The words NAVICVLARIORUM LIGNARIORVM advertise the office of shippers of wood. Others showed the professions of the tradesmen or the wares they were offering. Several indicate that there was a regular run of ships between Ostia and a number of cities in the western Mediterranean. (Travel to the eastern Mediterranean usually began in Brindisi, on the eastern coast of Italy.) Sailors would normally load their ships with amphorae or other vessels filled with fine wine or olive oil and return with grain, *garum* (a popular fish sauce) or other products from distant cities.

Mining

Controlling the sources of precious or useful metals was as important for the Romans as it had been for the Phoenicians, on the eastern end of the Mediterranean, and later the Carthaginians. Carthage, on the north coast of Africa in modern-day Tunisia, had been a serious threat to the Romans in the fourth to second centuries BC, as well as a competitor for raw materials such as silver and copper. Domination of the seas meant that trade routes were opened and precious commodities were ensured. The Etruscan cities of Populonia and

56 Water wheel. Wood. From the Rio Tinto copper mines, Spain.

Vetulonia, and the island of Elba, too, had abundant metal sources. Ancient peoples needed metal, especially for weapons and coinage, both of which became ever more important as Rome expanded.

The mines in Spain that produced gold, silver and especially copper passed to the Romans after their effective conquest of Carthage in 202/1 BC. Continued exploitation of the mines required additional mechanical ingenuity to cope with the universal problem of flooding. Part of a reconstituted mechanism for draining the mines can be seen in the pieces of a wooden wheel with a series of box-like scoops at the perimeter (**fig. 56**). The piece described here came from the Rio Tinto mines in northwest Spain, where one of the most elaborate linked systems raised the water nearly 100 feet (30.4 metres).[11] The wheel was made with pairs of flat spokes at each side of a relatively narrow series of boards that were bent to form the rims. The exterior of the wheel served as a treadmill. As the wheel turned, the scoops would fill with water towards the bottom of its travel and then carry it up to a tipping point just past the highest point of the circle, where the water would spill out into a trough or basin. This could then be directed to another revolving wheel to repeat the manoeuvre. Each of the wheels raised the water another 12 feet (3.6 metres) or so.

Labouring in the mines was one of the hardest and most dangerous occupations in the Roman world. The miners were usually criminals convicted of serious offences and sentenced to hard labour in the mines (*ad metalla*) – the equivalent of a lingering death sentence. Most of the time the mines were a government monopoly but operated by contractors (the hated *publicani*) who had bid for the privilege of running them. They had, therefore, every incentive to squeeze the last ounce of energy from the workmen to get back their investment and, beyond that, to make a handsome profit. Physical evidence in the mines themselves shows that the galleries were narrow and not very tall, the rock hard, and the lighting from just a few oil lamps (see p. 83) inadequate. The best evidence for this comes from the Rio Tinto mines, but we can be sure that it was the same for other mines all over the Roman world. Post-excavation processing like crushing, that leaves tailings (unprocessed parts of the ore), and smelting (that leaves a residue of slag) seems to have taken place near the source of the ore. The ingots of metal would then be distributed to brokers and sold as required.

Irrigation

Water was important, among other things, for the irrigation of grape vines and other crops. When authorized (and even when not authorized), some of the supply was siphoned off along the course of the aqueducts or rivers, using either gravity or water-raising devices to get the water where it was needed.

A device for raising water, described by the Roman architect Vitruvius (10.6), was especially useful for the quantity of water raised rather than the height achieved. It works on the principle of the screw; indeed it is often known as 'Archimedes' Screw' because a Greek mathematician and engineer by that name is thought to have invented it.[12] (Archimedes lived in the third century BC and came from Syracuse in Sicily.) Simple versions are still in use in many parts of the world without access to power, and the principle is used even on sophisticated machinery in industrialized countries. A spiral flange is constructed around a cylinder and is inserted into another cylinder to make a snug but not too tight fit (**fig. 57**). The inner cylinder is provided with a handle so that it can be turned within the outer cylinder. The whole thing is set at an angle of about 30 degrees with the bottom submerged in the water source. When the inner cylinder is turned, water is forced up and along the flange, which prevents it from escaping, and as the rotation continues, more water is forced in and pushes the original water up towards the top, where it spills out into a basin or an irrigation ditch.

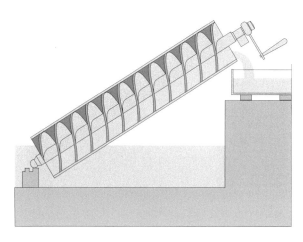

57 Diagram of Archimedes' Screw, a kind of water pump.

The Romans made use of a pump where the water could be taken in at one end and forced up and out through pipes by the action of a piston or a pair of pistons linked to a rocking beam (**fig. 58**). As one piston rose in its sleeve, it drew in water past a simple flap-like valve. Then, as it was pushed down again, the pressure forced the intake valve shut, causing the water to flow under pressure out of another valve that was hinged in the opposite way. Two pistons, accurately turned for a tight fit and greased, could be connected by being attached to either end of the same beam pivoting in the middle, and the seesaw action would double the capacity of the pump.[13] This type had a limited capacity and was more suitable for domestic applications such as garden fountains.

Section through
lower part of piston

Water level

58 A double-action water pump. *c.* third century AD. From Bolsena. H. 25.4 cm, W. 33 cm (10 x 13 in).

The amenities enjoyed by Roman citizens and the free inhabitants of the empire were in many cases derived from public works initiated and paid for by influential magistrates. Roman authors often allude to buildings provided *pro bono publico* (for the public good). Ostentatious, competitive spending was not a part of early Roman tradition, but gradually, with the concentration of great wealth in private hands in the late Republic, conspicuous consumption became common, and nobles were prone to excesses of every kind. This wealth had been accumulated through the plunder of other places such as Greece, Sicily and Carthage, which had been rich areas for centuries.

From small objects to major engineering projects, the Romans were extremely practical and had the ability to put technology to use in innumerable ways. The labour involved was typically performed by slaves, some of whom were highly skilled at their trades. Yet it was the imagination and expertise of Roman patrons and overseers, seeking to improve their own status and advancement, that brought about such remarkable accomplishments.

4

Coinage and Commerce

It would be hard to overstate the huge impact the Roman network of trade and commerce had on its far-flung empire. Partly due to the vastly improved road system that criss-crossed Europe, the Middle East and North Africa, and also as a result of extensive shipping, products easily reached distant lands. The influence of trade affected relationships between peoples who previously had no contact with each other. Whether speaking about coinage and mints, or large-scale movement of raw materials such as required by the marble trade, the effect of Roman commerce was to last for centuries.

Coinage

Commerce in Italy before the coming of the Greeks in the seventh and sixth centuries BC was carried out largely through the exchange of lumps of copper that formed the basis for the earliest Roman coinage. In fact, this form of exchange at Rome does not fit the usual definition of 'coinage', in that the lumps are not marked nor are they of uniform weight. This *aes rude* ('rough copper'), as it is called, is really no more than the broken and shapeless pieces of the ingot produced at the tapping of the furnace (**fig. 59**): only their occurrence in hoards points to their use as currency.

The mechanism for valuing these pieces still remains a matter of speculation and must somehow be harmonized with the fact that the standard Latin word for money was *pecunia*, which must be closely related to *pecus*, 'a herd of cattle'; thus, clearly, animals were used as a measure of wealth that was also common in prehistoric Greece. The particular animal used as a yardstick depends upon the culture in question: cattle or camels come to mind as continuing examples, even today.

After much discussion over the years, something like consensus has been reached that has the Romans and their neighbours facilitating trade or making payments through the medium of copper bullion, weighed as necessary. This corresponds to the *aes rude* mentioned above, and to a series of rectangular bars with cast designs on them, known as *aes signatum*, marked copper (**fig. 60**). These bars, used in the early third century BC, were generally heavier than the shapeless lumps of *aes rude*. The piece illustrated has a pig on one side and an elephant on the other. The latter may refer to the elephants brought to Italy by

59 *Aes rude*. Two sides of a lump of copper. H. 29 mm (1⅛ in).

60 *Aes signatum*, or money ingot, with an elephant on one side and a pig on the other. Copper. Early third century BC. L. 17 cm (6.7 in), Wt. 1.746 kg.

the Greek king Pyrrhus, who used them to aid in his fight against the Romans in 280 BC. The elephants played a role in a battle in which great losses were suffered on both sides, and led to the term 'pyrrhic victory', where one wins the battle but loses the war.

Rome's expanding influence among the Greek cities of southern Italy brought its traders into continuous contact with more sophisticated systems of weights and measures. Part of the Greek commercial system for urban and rural life, as far back as the sixth century BC, included a more developed level of coinage based on a silver standard whose units already had a well-defined series of fractions. Appreciating the historical circumstances of contact with the Greeks in South Italy has led to the conclusion that the Romans created a silver coinage for circulation in this area. They used the local standard and style and very likely local design and production, but added the word *Romano* (short for *Romanorum*) to the coins to signify that the Romans issued them.

Thus, quite a few pieces with inscriptions identify towns in central Italy as the issuing authority, but nevertheless have a close physical affinity with the earliest cast pieces that have been classed as coins, the *aes grave* ('heavy copper') series (**fig. 61**). A standard coin, called an *as*, was initially one Roman pound, or twelve ounces (0.4 g.) of copper (although this was gradually reduced).[1] Smaller denominations were also made, in the amounts of one-half, one-third, one-quarter, one-sixth and one-twelfth of a pound. Later, in the third century BC, the *aes grave* (and subsequently the first conventionally struck Roman coppers) showed a marked reduction in the variety of reverse types. Possibly in response to the naval successes of Rome that ended the First Punic War, in 241 BC, all displayed the prow of a ship as the reverse type. On bronze coins this would become the mainstay stock type, particularly for the *as*, during Republican times. Indeed, even when the prow design had long ceased, throughout the imperial period, the Roman expression for a coin toss (flipping a coin) remained 'heads or ship' (*capita aut navia*). The other side of the coins, depending on the fractions they represented, had different gods and goddesses as types and letters or raised dots as marks of value. The illustration shows an *as* (marked with I); a half *as*; a third of an *as*, shown with four dots, representing four ounces out of twelve; and a quarter of an *as*, shown with three dots; a sixth with two dots; and a twelfth [or *uncia*, from which comes our word ounce] with one. The half *as* is marked with 'S' for semis, meaning 'half', instead of six dots.

Romans also coined money in silver to match the needs and weight standards of the Greek cities of southern Italy that they were bringing into their orbit through a mixture of strategic alliances and military conquest. Thus, they made several types of silver coins weighing as much as the *didrachms*, or two drachma pieces, of the Greek cities that had originally been founded as colonies several centuries earlier. Some of their names are familiar today, as Naples (*Neapolis*) or

61 Several examples of *aes grave* coins. Top to bottom and left to right: an *as*; a *semis*; a third of an *as*; a quarter of an *as*; a half-*as*; and an *uncia*. From Rome, *c.* 241–235 BC.

Paestum (*Poseidonia*). The introduction of a standard silver coin at Rome itself has been placed at 212/211 BC, not long after the making of the *as* in cast bronze.

The earliest types for this long-lived series of silver coins consisted of a head of Roma (goddess of Rome) wearing a winged helmet on the obverse or 'heads' side, and the Dioscuri (the twins Castor and Pollux) armed and riding horses on the reverse or 'tails' side. Castor and Pollux were chosen as counterparts to Roma as a reference to the belief that the divine twins had miraculously appeared at the battle of Lake Regillus (499 BC) where the Romans were doing badly against the Latins, and rescued them from defeat.

Behind the heads are the differing marks of value: X (*denarius* = 10 *asses*), V (*quinarius* = 5 *asses*), IIS (*sestertius* = 2½ *asses*). It is significant that the Roman unit of account was the *sestertius*, the equivalent of two and a half *asses* or one- quarter of a *denarius*, the standard silver coin at Rome. Prices, income and degrees of wealth were reckoned in *sestertii* rather than in larger units like the silver *denarius* or, later under the empire, the gold *aureus*. This results in remarkably high numbers even for quite mundane sums of money. Even the invention of a word that was the lexical equivalent of 1000 *sestertii* (the *sestertium*) still produced very large numbers. Of course, many of the transactions described could not be carried out in this denomination because of the inconvenience and the huge number of actual coins that would be required.

The contents of the coin hoards found over the years around the Roman empire confirm the opinion that the gold coins in particular should be seen as the primary medium for settling the accounts described in the written record. Finds of silver coins from the Roman era are not so common, but silver is subject to serious corrosion when buried in damp ground and may have been lost.

Paying soldiers is one of the keys to the development and use of coined money. The emergence of a Roman silver coinage in areas other than Rome and fitted to the local standards seems to confirm this usage. Repeated large payments of small amounts require a readily convertible instrument like a coin series with multiple units and fractions for day-to-day purchases like bread or cheese. According to the Roman historian Dio Cassius (53.11), regular soldiers in AD 69 were paid 300 *denarii* per year and the Praetorian Guard (a special unit in Rome) received double that amount.

Paying taxes required considerable quantities of coin in circulation, even though some taxes, especially on farmers, were assessed and delivered in kind. Many transport taxes, or *vectigalia*, as they were called, were levied on the spot like transport vehicle tolls or import–export duties. Access to sources of metal was important for many reasons, not the least of which was making coins. Spain in particular was an immediate target because of its large reserves of useful resources in the form of copper and silver.

Commerce

The Romans' success against the Carthaginians in the second century BC gave them access to the whole of the western Mediterranean. They were not content merely to trade, but were interested in taking control of the areas opened up by the Carthaginians before them. As the area of the Mediterranean world under Roman rule or influence expanded, existing trade networks were taken over and widened to take advantage of the new territory as well as any particular resources or manufactured products that became available. Where Roman forts, *castra*, were created, a permanent occupation centre often sprang up to cater to the soldiers' tastes, and eventually these centres would become towns, many of which survive to this day. In England, many such towns have *-chester* or *-caster*

Hoxne coin hoard

Among the many treasures in the hoard found by accident in 1992 at Hoxne, Suffolk, is a huge number of late fourth and early fifth century coins. Of the 14,780 coins found, 565 are gold *solidi*, that is thin gold coins weighing about 4 grammes. The *solidus*, which replaced the gold *aureus*, was first minted by Constantine I in AD 309–10. Most of those in the hoard were minted between AD 394 and 405, although all told they were struck in thirteen different mints under eight different emperors. The vast majority of coins in this hoard – 14,191 – are silver, mostly *siliquae* that date from Constantine II (ruled AD 337–40) to Constantine III (AD 407–11), a British pretender. In silver, again thirteen mints are represented under thirteen different emperors. Just a few of the coins are low value bronze *nummi*.[2]

The survival of so many silver coins, most of which usually corrode in the soil, is distinctly unusual. Nearly all the coins had been clipped, that is, the edges had been cut away so as to use the silver fragments to make forgeries. But the emperor's head is always left intact. The coins, together with other precious objects, were deposited in a wooden crate that did not survive beyond its metal fittings.

62 Coins in the Hoxne hoard. Found in 1992 at Hoxne, Suffolk.

63 Amphora for *garum*, fish sauce. Clay. First century AD. Said to be from Rome, but made in Spain. H. 91 cm (*c.* 3 ft).

at the end of the name, for example Winchester or Lancaster. In Arabic, too, the word *qasr*, meaning fortification or palace, often indicates an origin as a Roman camp, *castrum*.

Some of the best evidence for commerce in the neighbourhood of the forts can be found in the type of amphora used to transport exotic substances that soldiers might have known from their places of origin or last posting. Amphorae can be traced to their source by the composition of the clay and sometimes by explicit stamps on the handles. Some shapes were favoured for a single product such as the amphora that was used for transporting bulk quantities of the pungent fermented fish sauce known as *garum* (**fig. 63**). The trade in *garum* was a considerable industry on the Mediterranean coast of Spain and North Africa. Although the organic material itself may have been lost, the distribution of the ceramic containers beyond the manufacturing area sheds light on commerce and taste. Amphorae found in abundance are testimony to the widespread trade of liquid goods, specifically wine and olive oil in addition to *garum*. Certain kinds of amphorae had a second life when they were reused in the vaulting of late Roman roofs.

One of the major imports to Rome and other major cities was large quantities of exotic coloured marble brought in from quarries in Egypt, North Africa and Asia Minor, and white marble from Greece. Although small quarries existed in many places, these imports supplied the high quality building material for the sumptuous baths and other public and private structures of the Roman empire. Indeed the marble trade is in itself an area of study that has produced fascinating results. The tool marks still left on stones at quarries and those on cut stones have enabled scholars to determine, for instance, that marble in North Africa was quarried in large square blocks and then sliced into thin slabs to make veneer at the final site, after having been shipped long distances. On the other hand, hugely bulky elements such as columns and sarcophagi were trimmed more or less to their final shape at the quarry to reduce the weight for shipment. Masons' marks on column drums and other blocks were used to identify and count a worker's output when the stone had been finally prepared for use. These marks were normally not visible to the public, but would be placed on a part of the stone that would go flush up against another block.

One of the ways in which the trade in marble can be documented is through sarcophagi (see chapter 8). These stone coffins were often carved from marble that had travelled great distances, especially from quarries in Asia Minor. Typically the block would be hollowed out and trimmed to save weight, but the quarryman knew what kinds of decoration would be carved by the finishing mason, and thus he would leave rough projections for garlands, medallions and figures in the appropriate places on the roughed out shape. At the final site, his unknown 'collaborator' would carve the details on the projections left for him.

Government contracts made up a sizeable proportion of the commerce that passed to Italy through the port of Ostia to Rome. In particular, large quantities of corn and oil were necessary for the free distribution of foodstuffs to the urban plebeian population. Until the time of the emperor Claudius (AD 41–54), cargoes had been transferred to smaller vessels at Puteoli (the modern Pozzuoli near Naples) because the anchorage at Ostia was unsafe for the large corn ships coming from Sicily and later from Egypt. Claudius began a huge project of a partly excavated harbour basin surrounded by an enormous concrete mole, using the hulls of overturned cargo ships as the moulds. The details of this massive new construction only came to light as a result of the excavations for the lengthening of the runway of Leonardo da Vinci airport near Rome.

The harbour was actually dedicated in AD 64 by Claudius' successor Nero, who took credit for these public works by issuing a spectacular coin to commemorate the event (**fig. 64**). His brass *sestertius* depicts a birdseye view of the harbour with seven ships surrounded by warehouses and individual boat docks. A lighthouse with a standing figure on top gives warning of a new navigation hazard or signals the entrance to a more protected anchorage. A reclining Neptune with a ship's steering oar and a dolphin gives a sense of place to the scene. Two of the ships are distinctly smaller than the others and have no mast stepped; they must be the lighters to take the crop up river to its final destination. The place is specifically identified by the abbreviated inscription POROST just below Neptune combined with AVGVSTI directly over the lighthouse. This is short for Portus Ostiensis Augusti, 'the Augustan harbour of Ostia'. (In this case the Augustus was the emperor Nero who issued the coin, rather than the founder of the principate.) It was actually known as Portus (harbour) to distinguish it from the older anchorage in the mouth of the river. This usage corresponds to referring to 'the city' when one actually means the capital or largest town of the country one inhabits, like London, Paris or New York.

64 Coin of Nero showing the harbour at Ostia. Bronze *sestertius*. Mid-first century BC. Diam. 34 mm (1⅜ in).

These provisions at Ostia seem to have been adequate until the time of Trajan, who built an addition in the form of a hexagonal basin surrounded by warehouses a little further inland from the harbour of Claudius, and connected to it by a canal. The arrangement of the harbours is well reflected in Juvenal's description of the arrival of a ship into port:

At last the vessel entered the harbour of Ostia, passing the Tyrrhenian lighthouse, gliding between those massive piers that reach out to embrace the deep, and leave Italy far behind – a man-made breakwater that no natural harbour could equal. The captain nursed his lame vessel through to the inner basin, its waters so still that a rowboat could safely ride there. ...[3]

65 Markets of Trajan, Rome. AD 100–112.

Trajan, too, thought his public works deserved a coin, and in his version the image shows what is mostly an aerial view of the buildings with the warehouses flattened at the edges, much like a simplified engineering drawing rather than a pictorial rendering. These harbours were suitable for the very large ships that brought grain or corn to feed the people of Rome. The ships were too large to sail up the Tiber, so the cargo had to be offloaded into smaller boats to be taken upstream to the city.

Markets

Markets could be local and rural, such as the stalls that must have been set up in forums in every small town; or they could be elaborate and urban, like the Markets of Trajan in Rome (**fig. 65**). This complex abutted the Forum of Trajan, one of the imperial fora that were built near the ancient Republican Forum that had grown too small for the expanding city. Trajan's Forum had huge semi-circular exedrae on each side, an architectural feature that in itself mimicked the niches that had distinguished the Forum of Augustus a century earlier. Built around one of the exedrae of Trajan's Forum was the complex of shops, roads, and public spaces that became the Markets of Trajan.

At the ground level of Trajan's Forum, in a semi-circle, were shops with large doors and small windows above – the typical configuration of Roman stores. By ascending steps between the shops, one could attain the next level where a road, nicknamed 'Pepper Street' in modern times (Via Biberatica) bends around to follow the shape of the exedra and proceeds beyond the market in two directions. All told, five storeys make up the market, which was cut out of the hill above the forum. A contemporary inscription on Trajan's commemorative column announces that the height cut away was 100 [Roman] feet (= slightly more than 100 English feet, a little over 30 metres). The highest two levels are made up of more shops and a large roofed public space called the Aula, itself surrounded by two storeys of shops or offices.

The complex would have drawn people from all over the city and must have formed the hub of commercial life in Rome during the early second century AD. Carts moving through the streets would have made an unbearable clatter, caricatured by the satirist Juvenal (p. 54);[4] but in fact it was Trajan who passed a law limiting wagon traffic in the city to those carrying building materials, and even those were allowed to pass only at night. The Markets of Trajan were as sophisticated a set of commercial buildings as ever constructed in the Roman world.

Agricultural commerce

Implements used for farming or in industry were usually made of iron. A sickle would have been used to cut crops such as wheat, and a billhook (**fig. 66**) would have been attached with rivets to a wooden handle and used to trim branches and for pruning. Roman tools, as well as iron pickaxes and shears, are typical finds, and are hardly different from those used today by peasant farmers.

The use of draught animals for ploughs and carts was commonplace in ancient times. Wagons with solid wooden wheels would be drawn to market by

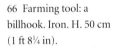

66 Farming tool: a billhook. Iron. H. 50 cm (1 ft 8¼ in).

67 Relief of oxcart going to market. Marble. Third century AD. H. 35.5 cm, W. 61 cm (1 ft 2 in x 2 ft).

68 Relief with man sailing a *corbita*. H. 23 cm, W. 61 cm (9 in x 2 ft).

oxen and would be loaded with produce. One illustrative relief (**fig. 67**) shows the cart bearing a large wineskin confined by stakes. Someone at the right (now mostly missing) prods one of the oxen with a stick, and a dog follows along underfoot. An eager-looking man with hand raised seems to greet the cart under an arch or gateway. A scene such as this could have been seen until recently in many countries around the Mediterranean. Other loads like timber and marble are specifically referred to in Juvenal's *Satire* (3.255–60) where he worries about the potential damage and casualties if the axle should break and the load tumble down on the crowd.

Another way of moving goods was by water. It was usually faster and cheaper because much bigger loads could be accommodated. A small marble relief (**fig. 68**) shows a man at the helm of a *corbita*, a slow merchant ship propelled by sails; this one has two. Both of them show indications of sewn panels and extra strengthening where the control ropes are attached; waves are indicated but there is no sign of any cargo projecting above the gunwales. The helmsman looks out at the viewer directly, with eyes that are outlined on the flat surface of the stone, as is frequent in Roman reliefs of the second century and later. In addition, the rather abrupt transitions in the carving from the frontal plane to the back mark this as coming from the less sophisticated provinces rather than one of the metropolitan centres.

Making wine was a widespread industry in rural areas. On the lid of a marble sarcophagus (**fig. 69**), a vat of new wine, or 'must', is shown being heated on a log fire at the left. A kneeling man lifts the lid to peek underneath, and a second man runs up, carrying sticks for the fire. The cooking of the wine will turn it into *defructum*, which could be drunk as new wine, or saved to make a concentrated 'must' with a jelly-like consistency. Some would be put in large casks to be fermented for nine days, after which it would be sealed shut in the jars.[5] On the right, a man is pouring wine from an amphora into a large basin from which the man on his left will fill his jug. Perhaps the subject indicates that the dead person will continue to enjoy his wine in the afterlife.

Measurements

The steelyard is often used today in places without modern equipment, or where precision is not of great importance, or for large or awkward items, particularly sides of meat or big sacks of produce. In fact, though, the Romans tried to get their measurements right, and merchants were required to give their clients fair value. The bronze steelyard (a weighing device distinct from a balance) illustrated has two positions, one for delicate measurements and the other for gross ones (**fig. 70**). The diamond shaped beam of a steelyard is usually suspended from a hook and pivots at a fulcrum so that one part is longer than the other. This means that a light weight can exert the force of a heavier one. As the weight is moved along the beam the force exerted at the end being weighed is multiplied by the ratio of the long end to the short end. In our example the whole beam is 34.5 cm (13½ in) long and the proportion of the long part to the short is about 1:15. The balance is hung so that the weight exerts the maximum force. If the steelyard were turned over, the ratio of the longer part to the shorter would be diminished and the same weight (in this case a helmeted head of

69 Lid of a sarcophagus with winemaking scene. Marble. Probably third century AD. H. 15 cm, W. 53 cm (6 in x 1 ft 9 in).

70 Steelyard. Bronze.
L. of arm: 33 cm (13 in).

Athena with a griffin crest) would produce less force and the balance could be used to handle a smaller load. These weights are moved along the arm, depending on the weight of the object. This example has a flat pan suspended by chains for holding the material to be weighed, but other devices could be attached to the ring in the end of the beam as appropriate. The horizontal bar has markings to show the poundage and also has many V-shaped nicks at fixed intervals to stop the weight slipping.

A much more complicated example (**fig. 71**) had three hooks, each attached to one face of the bar that could weigh up to 60 Roman pounds using one sliding weight. Greater precision could be obtained using a balance with equal arms and a set of predetermined weights in one of the pans, but that entailed fussing with multiples and fractions of the Roman pound (*libra*, which is the

71 Pair of scales with two pans. Bronze. The chains are modern. L. of arm: 24 cm (9½ in).

equivalent of about 324 grammes). The word is still with us in the symbol for the pound sterling, and is used for the weight of a pound in French, Italian, Spanish, Portuguese and Romanian.

Distant lands

Roman commerce involved trade with a huge international market, ranging from Spain in the west to India in the east. Arretine pottery (see p. 130) made in Italy has been found in South India, and Roman gold coins turn up as far away as China, where obtaining silk was the primary object. However, it seems that silk came through foreign traders, and so far as we know the Romans themselves did not get to China.

India was another story. Spices were dry, and did not take up much bulk; hence they were easy to transport from far distant lands.[6] However, they were expensive, and most were used only by the uppermost levels of society, who could make payments for spices in gold. Exotic spices from as far away as Indonesia were often mixed with local herbs, and would both liven up the food at banquets and mask the taste of items that might have been going off. Pepper, specifically, was widely sought after, and the importance of the sea route to South India cannot be overstated. Once this had been established, pepper was shipped to the farthest reaches of the empire, even to soldiers defending the northern flank at Hadrian's Wall,[7] and added an important element to the Roman diet. The spice trade stands as testimony to the long arm of Roman trade and to its contacts with people at the edges of the known world.

5

Spectacle and Entertainment

The Romans, great fans of entertainment, came to expect public spectacles almost as a civic right to be bestowed upon them by their ruler. The very notion of public entertainment began with the theatre where, in the Republican period, wealthy families would sponsor dramas. These were often in the context of a religious festival or a commemoration of a major event, such as a death. Eventually the sponsorship of public events fell to the emperor, who used such events for propaganda and the imperial agenda.

The Romans were addicted to large-scale public events that frequently involved the shedding of blood of both animals and humans. Also the danger of the activity, ranging from gladiatorial fights to chariot racing, seems to have added to the appeal. *Panem et circenses*, 'bread and circuses' was a phrase invented by the Roman satirist Juvenal to express his disdain for handouts of free foodstuffs and entertainment.

> Now that no one buys our votes, the public has long since cast off its cares; the people that once bestowed commands, consulships, legions, and all else, now meddles no more and longs eagerly for just two things – bread and circuses.[1]

The year was filled with an inordinate number of holidays, 159 in the time of Claudius, and of these, 93 were dedicated to games paid for by the public purse.[2] Emperors used this expectation to satisfy the citizens, and to gain popularity. By making such offers, including horse racing, gladiatorial fights and even sea battles in public arenas, they bribed the public to support them. From Republican times onwards, structures such as amphitheatres, race courses and theatres became standard features of Roman towns.

Amphitheatres

The tradition of gladiatorial combat may have come from Southern Italian or Etruscan funeral ceremonies. Gladiators were men who fought each other with weapons in a formal competition, a little like fencing but almost always with a fatal outcome. In a gladiatorial combat, if one participant was not already killed during the action, his fate would be decided by the attitude of the crowd or the

72 Lamp with two
gladiators. Clay.
c. 15 BC–AD 15.
L. 14 cm (5½ in).

emperor: the judgment was expressed in a gesture that has become known as 'thumbs up' or 'thumbs down', to determine whether the life of the less skilful combatant would be spared or not. If the life of the loser was to be saved, the crowd would shout *missum*, meaning 'discharged', and people would raise their left hand or wave a cloth in the air; if he were to be killed, they would shout *jugula* ('slay') and turn their thumbs down.[3]

A typical scene is represented on a lamp with a victorious gladiator and a fallen one (**fig. 72**). A Thracian gladiator, identifiable by his small shield and greaves (leg protectors), stands over a fallen *murmillo* who awaits the ultimate verdict that will determine if he is to live or die. Gladiators were often common criminals and therefore considered dispensable, but many were professionally trained athletes and were valuable assets for their owners.

Spectacles usually took place in arenas that had different names, depending on their shape and the kind of event that was held there. Amphitheatres, oval-shaped with banked seats on all sides, were suitable for athletic events that ranged from gladiatorial competitions to artificial wild beast hunts. The word

73 The Colosseum, in Rome. AD 72–80. H. 48.5m, L. 188 m, W. 156 m (159 ft x 616 ft x 511 ft 10 in).

comes from an image of two theatres put together, front to front on the flat end: 'amphi' means 'on both sides' in Greek, and is used as in 'amphibious'. The Colosseum (**fig. 73**) was the largest amphitheatre anywhere, but large and small, these structures were a common feature of Roman towns.

The Colosseum had a huge capacity, estimated to hold about 50,000 spectators. Its seating was on a steep slant, only the foundations of which survive (although marble seats have been restored in one section). People would enter and leave the arena by the eighty exits that enabled them to move in and out quickly. The floor is now mostly missing, but the numerous underground passages where animals passed to and fro can still be seen. In fact, in addition to access via ramps, elevators on pulleys lifted the cages of the beasts from those passages to the level of the floor of the arena. Gladiators too used the tunnel-like walkways, and could reach their barracks that lay beyond the limits of the Colosseum by travelling underground.

The structure of the building is ingenious. Arched passageways and staircases allowed the spectators to move around the arena. The exterior is made up of four levels, each with supporting arches encircling the building. Decorative half-columns at the lower three levels, and pilasters on the top level, frame the arches but are not structural.

Such a huge building required great amounts of travertine, a kind of limestone that was (and still is) quarried in Tivoli, ancient Tibur. After one end of the Colosseum collapsed in an earthquake during the Middle Ages, it was used as a quarry for buildings of the Renaissance and beyond. The nicely squared blocks served beautifully for the palaces, churches, and public buildings being constructed over the centuries.

The American writer Mark Twain recorded his travels in *The Innocents Abroad* (1869) and has a fine description of how the Colosseum looked in the nineteenth century:

Everybody knows the picture of the Colosseum; everybody recognizes at once that 'looped and windowed' bandbox with a side bitten out [where the stones fell in the earthquake]. Being rather isolated, it shows to better advantage than any other of the monuments of ancient Rome. … Weeds and flowers spring from its massy arches and its circling seats, and vines hang their fringes from its lofty walls. An impressive silence broods over the monstrous structure where such multitudes of men and women were wont to assemble in other days. …[4]

Amphitheatres and violent spectacles were common in Asia Minor (the Greek east of the Roman empire) as well as in the west, and a large graveyard for gladiators was found at Ephesus.[5] It was in the amphitheatres that most violent

Rounding up animals for the amphitheatre

The collection of wild beasts was mostly concentrated in North Africa and Asia Minor where appropriate animals could be found. A mosaic depicting just such a hunting scene, and serving as the floor of an apse to a dining room, comes from Tunisia. It shows the rounding up of animals and birds in a net: a boar, stag, wild dog, ostrich, gazelle, leopard, lizards and birds. Two naked men in a boat on the left, and another pair on the right, all hold the ends of a dragnet that curves to fill the shape of the mosaic. Apparently a flood has cornered the animals, and the men have taken advantage of the situation by going out in boats. Eventually the captured beasts would be loaded on to ships at the nearest port and delivered to cities around the Mediterranean, especially Rome, where they would serve to entertain the throngs in the amphitheatre. The animals would be set to fight against each other, or they would be hunted by *venatores* (hunters) in the amphitheatres.

74 Mosaic showing the capturing of animals for the arena. AD 200–225. From Utica, Tunisia. H. 1.51 m, L. 3.32 m (5 x 11 ft).

events took place, including fights between men, or between men and animals. Staged hunts of exotic or dangerous animals were popular from late Republican times to the first century BC, when the sponsorship of these events was a mechanism for bringing candidates for office to public attention. The orator Cicero reported that he was asked to procure some large felines (*pantherae*), of an undetermined species, while he was governor in Cilicia – in what is now southern Turkey.[6] In imperial times the sponsorship of the games became a prerogative of the emperor, but with something of the same purpose: to gain (or retain) the favour of the populace.

ABOVE 75 Helmet of a
murmillo (gladiator).
Bronze. First century AD.
Said to be from Pompeii.
H. 46 cm (1 ft 8 in),
Wt. 3.6 kg (8 lb).

ABOVE RIGHT
76 A *retiarius* (gladiator).
Bronze. H. 6.25 cm (2½ in).

Like the Colosseum, many smaller amphitheatres have passageways underground through which the animals would be moved before emerging on to the platform or floor of the arena. Gates were specifically tailored for different animals. Just as the fights between wild beasts could be varied by the choice of animal, so too combat between gladiators could be varied by the equipment they carried. A *retiarius* did not wear a helmet, but carried a three-pronged trident and a net that he tried to throw over his adversary (**fig. 76**). A *murmillo*, or heavily armed gladiator, wore an elegant helmet with a grille made of linked circles of bronze through which he could see (**fig. 75**). A large overhanging flange protected his head on all sides, including the back. The heavy helmet in the British Museum, weighing approximately 8 pounds (3.6 kg), was decorated with a high crest that would have had feathers attached to it. A medallion of Hercules wearing the lion skin tied under his neck decorates the front above the visor. Needless to say, the strongman hero Hercules would symbolize courage and strength as well as victory. The *murmillo*'s other equipment included padded linen arm and leg bands.

77 Relief of two female gladiators. Marble. First–second century AD. From Halicarnassus (modern Bodrum), Turkey. H. 66 cm, W. 78 cm (2 ft 2 in x 3 ft 1 in).

A marble relief from Halicarnassus depicts an unusual scene: a fight between two female gladiators, each wielding a sword and a shield (**fig. 77**). The inscription indicates that the relief commemorates the retirement from service of the two women, 'Amazon' and 'Achilia'. They are shown bare-headed, but it is likely that the objects at the bottom corners may be their helmets if they are not spectators. Contemporary writers commented on female gladiators, confirming that these two were not unique,[7] but this slab is the only piece of solid archaeological evidence for their existence.

On the one hand were the public spectacles held in the amphitheatres where gladiators fought with gladiators, or where beasts fought with beasts. On the other were public executions where criminals who had been condemned to death were forced to go into the amphitheatre where they were set upon by wild beasts, a practice that was responsible for the expression, 'being thrown to the lions'. This is the spectacle that inspired the miraculous story of 'Androcles and the Lion', told in antiquity by Aulus Gellius (*Noctes Atticae* 5.14) and Aesop, and serving as the inspiration for a play of the same title by George Bernard Shaw. It tells of a slave, Androcles, who escapes from his master into the wilderness. He is terrified as a lion comes up to him, roaring with pain as he holds up one foot. Androcles discovers that a thorn has infected the lion's paw, and pulls it out. After that the lion becomes a devoted friend, bringing food to the slave and looking after him. Eventually Androcles is captured, and brought back to his master who decides to throw him to the lions for having run away. To everyone's amazement, in the arena, the lion rushes out but instead of killing him, he falls at his feet. It was of course the same lion. As a reward for this remarkable event, the slave and the lion were both set free.

The circus

In contrast to amphitheatres, the circus, known to the Greeks as a hippodrome, was a long and narrow race course for chariot races. In the absence of a dedicated structure, it could be turned into a venue for gladiators and wild beast fights, and in rare instances it could be converted into a place for mock sea battles. Chariot racing was established early in Roman history and was

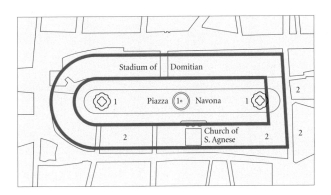

78 Diagram of the Stadium of Domitian, overlayed by the Piazza Navona, Rome.

79 Piazza Navona, Rome, located over the Stadium of Domitian.

associated with day-long events that took place as part of religious observances. It may have derived from the Greeks, particularly from those towns in Sicily where several victors in the Olympic games are recorded in inscriptions and poetry. But Roman circuses were much more elaborate than the Greek hippodrome and had various new features. The shape, with one end straight across and the other end rounded, is found also in the Roman stadium that was constructed on a smaller scale, more appropriate for athletics and foot races. The shape of one has been preserved in the Piazza Navona in Rome, located over the Stadium of Domitian whose remains still rest beneath the modern buildings (**figs. 78 and 79**). It was constructed of arches made of large stone blocks, some of which can still be seen at one end of the structure under the level of the modern road. In fact, three of the steps discovered below one of the buildings explains the name, *Tre Scalini*, given to one of the most famous ice cream parlours in Rome. The space continued to be

80 A two-horse chariot, a *biga*. Bronze. Found in the River Tiber. H. 18 cm, L. 25 cm (7 in x 10 in).

used for athletic events long after the Roman empire had fallen, and indeed the words *Campus Agonis* ('athletic field') evolved into Piazza Navona. It has again been a centre for lively entertainment for the last several centuries.

Running down the centre of a Roman circus was a low wall, the *spina*, that divided the two straight sections of the track. At each of its ends were conical columns, or turning posts called *metae*, that the horses had to clear as they went around the corner. Another feature on the *spina* was a bar held up by two columns, and on this bar were placed egg-shaped balls, *ova,* to mark each of the rounds of the horses. That way both the charioteers and the crowd could keep track of the progress. The starting gates were lined up on a diagonal so that those on the outer lane would not have to go farther than those on the inner lane, who otherwise would have had a big advantage.

Typically a chariot would be drawn by two-horses, a *biga* (**fig. 80**) or by four horses, a *quadriga*. On the small bronze model representing a *biga*, only one of the two horses has survived and the charioteer too has been lost; but it is a splendidly lively piece that shows the horse galloping at high speed and records the construction of a racing chariot. It was made of wicker and leather, creating a lightweight structure above the small spoked wheels. A ram's head, preserved behind the horse's mane, decorates the yoke pole that connected the horses to the chariot.

On a brownish clay jar from Colchester in Essex (**fig. 81**), four *quadrigae* are racing around the exterior in a lively interpretation of a race. Each of the horses appears to be stretched to the full. Some of the figures that were put on free-

81 Pot with four four-horse chariots (*quadrigae*). Clay. From Colchester. H. 15 cm (6 in).

hand were applied when the clay was too dry, causing some sections of the relief to fall off without a trace of a scar at the join. An actual circus was found at Colchester in 2005.

The dangers in chariot racing stemmed from the speed and the crowded field of competitors, as well as the abrupt turn required at the end of the *spina*. The axles of the chariots tended to overheat and sometimes even caused the wooden hub to catch fire. The Latin poet Statius describes how 'the wheels of the racing chariot dash against each other'.[8] Friction was the most intense as the chariot rounded the end of the *spina*, and it was here that special attendants threw buckets of cold water on the wheels as the charioteer rushed by. An account of a spectacular wreck is recorded in Sophocles' *Electra*[9] where Electra's brother Orestes is said to be the doomed charioteer who grazed the turning post, which upset the delicate balance of the chariot; but the tutor or *paidagogos* who is telling the story passes on a false rumour as part of an ironic plot.

ANNIAE
ARESCVSA

82 Relief of a circus. Terracotta. Last third of the first century AD. H. 30.5 cm, L. 41 cm (12 x 16 in).

The potential for such accidents can be seen in a terracotta plaque[10] (**fig. 82**) showing a race around the turning place with the conical posts at the end of the *spina*. The four horses of the *quadriga* are being urged on by the charioteer, who holds a whip in one hand and has tied the reins around his waist. One charioteer has already fallen at the turning post, and a *jubilator* (someone who urges on the other drivers) can be seen at the far right, disappearing around the *meta*e. The charioteers would wear bright colours related to their sponsors so they could be easily distinguished from their competitors. The flavour – and danger – of the event as well as the fervour of the crowd reminds one of a modern motor car race.

Baths

Going to the baths was a social event among the Romans; they adapted and ultimately transformed the Greek institution of athletic competition and the requisite washing afterwards into a cultural habit where the athletic components were minimized and the social and sensual aspects became paramount. Washing oneself was not the prime object, even though people did want to get clean. Exercise and athletic competition took place in the palaestra (athletic fields), part of the bath complex.

Bathing involved luxurious warming, steaming and cooling oneself in finely decorated premises, all offering a high level of service and opportunity for socializing. Petronius describes a group of men attending the baths before the spectacular dinner hosted by Trimalchio (*Satyricon* 28):

> We quickly undressed, went into the hot baths, and, after working up a sweat, passed on to the cold showers. There we found Trimalchio again, his skin glistening all over with perfumed oil. He was being rubbed down, not with ordinary linen, but with cloths of the purest and softest wool. During this rubdown, right before his eyes, the three masseurs were guzzling away at the finest of his rare Falernian wines. ...[11]

It is amusing to read how one historian put it in the early twentieth century:

> The habits of luxury and inertia which were accentuated by the magnificent baths of the Emperors were among the causes of the decline of Rome, and the vices which were encouraged in the Baths found one reaction in the impression of the early Christians that uncleanliness was a virtue, an impression which is retained by certain Monastic Orders to the present day ... Thousands of the Roman youth frittered away their lives in these magnificent halls, which were provided with everything which could gratify the senses.[12]

Another tells us more about the excesses:

> While the bath was used for health merely or cleanliness, a single one was considered sufficient at a time, and that only when requisite. But the luxuries of the Empire knew no such bounds, and the daily bath was sometimes repeated as many as seven and eight times in succession – the number which the Emperor Commodus indulged himself with.[13]

83 Athlete with a strigil. Bronze. An Etruscan statuette of about 500–475 BC. From Arezzo. H. 10.5 cm (4¼ in).

The prime method used by an athlete to clean himself was to rub down his body with oil and then scrape himself to remove the sweat, dirt, dead skin and oil all at once. An Etruscan bronze statuette of an athlete scraping his thigh (**fig. 83**) illustrates how this was done, using a curved scraper called a *strigil*.[14] On the other hand, athletes, like other people, also cleaned themselves with water at the baths.

Baths were frequented by people of all classes, from the emperor to slaves, and although practices varied at different times and places, sometimes women and men bathed together, apparently naked.[15] It is not clear if slaves could

84 The Baths of Caracalla, Rome. AD 211–17. Concrete and brick with marble veneer.

normally bathe there, although it seems that they might have availed themselves of the opportunity while accompanying their masters.[16]

The largest baths in Rome were those built under Caracalla in the early third century AD (**fig. 84**). The baths themselves consisted of several different halls with pools, often symmetrically aligned on an axis and usually roofed. These would included a large rectangular cold bath, the *frigidarium*; a warm bath (*tepidarium*); and a small hot bath (*caldarium*) that might be round and rather like a plunge bath. In addition, an open-air *natatio*, or swimming pool, would be the last option, especially in the larger imperial bath complexes. People would often move from one pool to the another, lingering for refreshment and conversation along the way.

The methods of heating the *tepidarium* and *caldarium* were remarkable feats of engineering, used everywhere in the Roman world in baths large and small.

Under the floor would be a construction known as the *hypocaust*, which consisted of short pillars, the *pilae*, usually made of brick. Nearby, also below the floor level, would be a furnace that was stoked by a slave (or slaves, depending on the size of the baths). Working in the heat under the floors must have been truly dreadful. From this furnace the hot air would flow around the brick pillars, heating the water in the pools and even making the marble floors so hot that bathers had to wear shoes. The *caldarium* would be closest to the furnace, and the *tepidarium* the next room, a bit farther away. After the air had passed through the *hypocaust*, it would then escape through specially designed ducts, the *tubuli*, that would rise through the walls behind a marble facing and out into the open air above. Thus, the walls too would be warmed through the residual heat of the furnace air.

Each bath had a changing room, the *apodyterium*, where people would leave their clothes upon entering the complex. Cupboard-like niches would presumably have had doors and functioned like lockers. Normally there would be a separate changing room for men and for women, or else the facilities would have been designated for one or the other at different times of day.

Large baths, often known as imperial baths, offered many additional facilities that further enriched the possibilities for lounging and the pleasure of bathers. Among the amenities in these complexes would be a library where readers could choose from a wealth of scrolls that were stored in niches in the wall. Also available would be gardens, eateries, and other places for interaction. The large open areas for socializing at such baths would also have served for conducting business, albeit on a more informal basis than what would typically have transpired in the forum or basilica.

Theatres

Drama, and the theatres in which plays were seen, had been a staple of Greek society. Romans too were drawn to this form of entertainment, and Roman dramatists wrote plays inspired by Greek tragedies and comedies. However, the uneducated element in Roman audiences tended to be less interested in highbrow drama, and more in slapstick and bawdy entertainment. No matter what the play, the actors would wear masks with a comic or tragic facial expression, depending on the subject matter (**fig. 85**). In this relief, two masks are seen, one tragic and one comic. The comic mask in front is bearded, and a wreath of fennel encircles the head. The face has a wildly exaggerated laughing mouth, widely open so that the voice of the actor could be heard by the audience. The tragic mask behind, in profile, has a down-turned mouth, also widely open. Holes were left at the eyes and nostrils as well as the mouth so the actor could see and breathe. Women were not allowed to be actors, so women's parts were played by men.

ABOVE 85 Relief with two theatre masks, one comic, one tragic. Marble. H. 23.5 cm (9¼ in).

As in amphitheatres and circuses, entrances in theatres were marked by numbers, and tickets were marked for specific sections. Tickets or tokens thought to have been used for entry to the seating areas survive, but little information remains about how they were procured or allotted. People normally had to pay, even if only a nominal amount. Roman theatres were often built up from the flat ground (**fig. 87**), as opposed to Greek theatres that were usually built into a hill. They had fairly steep rises to the highest seats where the poorer people generally sat. The seats themselves were actually long curved benches made of stone on which the theatre-goers would place their own pillows.

Popular formats in the Roman theatre of imperial times were the mime and the pantomime. While mime tended toward the bawdy, pantomime was somewhat more elevated. Both depended on gesture to get their messages across. The illustration (**fig. 86**) shows a group of three terracotta statuettes of men with grotesque features representing pantomimes acting out the plots with gestures, music and dance. The musicians who would usually accompany them are absent. Roman slapstick comedy and plots, best exemplified by the rollicking plays of Plautus in the third century BC, were often centered on mistaken identity and were to have a huge effect on later drama, from Shakespeare to Gilbert and Sullivan and the modern 'sit-com'.

RIGHT 86 Three actors. Terracotta. Perhaps from Izmir. H. 16–17 cm (c. 6½ in).

LEFT 87 Theatre of Marcellus, Rome. 13 BC. Travertine. Width of seating area: 111 m (360 ft).

6

Religions, Near and Far

Roman rituals, deep-seated and widely practised, were frequently maintained for centuries. While some of them went back to Etruscan or Greek times, others were particularly Roman. One of these was the so-called *suovetaurilia*, the sacrifice of a pig, a sheep and a bull. In fact the word is made from the three words *sus* (pig), *ovis* (sheep) and *taurus* (bull). Usually the three animals were shown together in a single relief, but here the three figurines do not actually go

88 Animals for the *suovetaurilia* sacrifice. First century BC or first century AD.
Sheep. Clay. Said to be from Syria. H. 12 cm (c. 5 in).
Pig. Bronze. Said to come from near Rome. H. 2.5 cm (1 in).
Bull. Clay. Said to come from Tarquinia. H. 11 cm (4¼ in).

together (**fig. 88**). Each has a garland or band around his head or body, readying him for sacrifice. The sheep has a garland with leaves on his head, above his twisted horns, and the texture of his woolly coat is shown by nicks in the clay. The pig has a band around his body, and the bull's body is encircled by a garland. Sometimes these three animals would be led around the farmer's fields before they were to be sacrificed, as a way of ensuring that the crops would be safe from pests. Furthermore, this rite was associated especially with the making of lists, particularly the five-yearly census of the Roman people. Many state events were accompanied by the taking of the auspices, which was the ritual slaying of animals and inspection of their entrails in order to decide whether to proceed with the ceremony. The sacrifice was thought to bring purification to the people.

Gods and goddesses

The polytheistic religion of the Romans allowed them to worship gods that ranged from all-powerful controllers of natural phenomena, such as lightning, earthquakes, or the sea, to gods involved with the most intimate and personal of human events, especially with women's concerns and gynaecological issues. Most of the major Roman gods had close parallels in Greek religion, although as time went on many eastern divinities were adopted into the Roman pantheon. Zeus, most powerful of the Greek gods and controller of thunder, was Jupiter to the Romans (**fig. 89**). As often, he holds a thunderbolt in his left hand (shown with a twisted point at both ends), representing his control over the skies in general and thunder in particular. Overlapping spheres of other deities were those of Aphrodite, Greek goddess of love, with the Roman Venus; Artemis, goddess of the hunt, with Diana; Ares, god of war, with Mars; among others (see Gods and Heroes, p. 186).

Diana and her twin brother Apollo are featured on one of the most spectacular silver pieces in the British Museum, the so-called Corbridge *Lanx*, or tray (**fig. 90**). A work from the fourth century AD, the tray was found in 1735 by a nine-year-old girl,

89 Statuette of seated Jupiter with sceptre and thunderbolt. Bronze. Found in Hungary. H. 18 cm (7 in).

90 Corbridge Lanx. Silver. From Corbridge. Fourth century AD. H. 48 cm, W. 38 cm (15 x 19 in).

91 Painting of Bacchus and Silenus. From a villa at Boscoreale. H. of Bacchus: 76 cm (2½ ft).

the daughter of a local blacksmith, on the banks of the River Tyne at Corbridge (ancient Coria). The story of its discovery sounds like the makings of a novel.[1]

The scene on the lanx takes place at a shrine of Apollo, who stands naked at the right, holding his bow in his left hand and a laurel sprig in his right. He had set his lyre against the column by his feet, probably at his shrine on the island of Delos. His sister Diana walks in from the left holding her bow and arrow. She is greeted by Minerva, helmeted and wearing a cuirass with Medusa on her chest. The identity of the two other women is uncertain. Below are Diana's hound, a fallen stag, an altar, and the griffin associated with Apollo. The scene, hammered out with skill, shows how classical themes were still being made in the manner of the early empire well into the fourth century. The full-bodied figures, naturalistic drapery, identity and attributes of the gods, and token tree and architecture all hark back to classical origins.

As in so many ancient religions, each god or goddess was responsible for an essential part of life or experience, from child-bearing (Juno) to vegetation (Ceres). Typically an attribute, such as the peacock for Juno or grain for Ceres, would be connected with the divinity and indeed the attribute could stand in for the goddess herself. The practice was to make offerings to the appropriate deity when his or her help was needed; in other words, by giving something, one expected to get something in return.

Bacchus (Dionysos to the Greeks), the god of wine, was one of the most beloved of Roman deities. He is often shown with a panther or leopard and with some of his retinue consisting of maenads, satyrs, and the elderly Silenus. A painting of a naked

92 Dionysus and a Panther.
Mosaic from a villa near
Halicarnassus. Fourth
century AD. Excavated by
C.T. Newton. H. 1.3 m,
W. 1.35 m (4 ft 3¼ in x 4 ft
5¼ in).

Bacchus, his leopard and Silenus comes from a villa at Boscoreale near Pompeii
(**fig. 91**). Appropriately enough, it had been painted on a pilaster to the right of
the entrance to the villa's wine press. A chubby and bearded Silenus, his lower
body draped, plays the lyre while the much larger Bacchus, holding a thin
thyrsus in his left hand, pours wine out of a cup for the leopard to drink. The
thyrsus, a giant fennel stalk topped by a pinecone, is sometimes decorated, as
here, with ribbons. Bacchus, maenads and satyrs all carried this item. Ivy leaves
decorate the heads of Bacchus, Silenus and the back of the panther and bunches
of grapes hang from a garland above. Consistent lighting from the right throws
shadows from their legs and helps to make the figures look three-dimensional.
As often in Roman painting, the brush strokes look fresh and spontaneous.

It is interesting to compare the painting with a mosaic of a dancing Dionysos
and his panther from a fourth-century AD villa near ancient Halicarnassus, now
Bodrum in Turkey (**fig. 92**). The heavy-thighed god, with green wreath, prances
along in step with the animal, and the red cloth he carries behind him flaps in
the wind, adding to the sense of movement. The mosaicist used black tesserae[2]
to outline the cloth and the god's face and legs. The panther's beard and the hair
on his legs are indicated with roughly parallel short black lines, and his spots are

black. The technique of laying stones for a mosaic usually makes the end result coarser and less precise than a painting. That is true here, but the mosaic is nonetheless successful and lively.

Another Bacchus and panther may be compared in a different medium. One of the greatest hoards of silver vessels found in Britain from the Roman period is the Mildenhall Treasure, discovered in 1942 by a ploughman in Suffolk. Consisting of thirty-three objects, the hoard may be dated to approximately the same period as the mosaic just mentioned. The great Mildenhall dish, 61 cm (2 ft) in diameter, has a bacchic theme, with Bacchus himself shown with his thyrsus in hand, standing with his sandalled foot on the back of the panther at his feet (**fig. 93**). Silenus offers the god a drink from a cup. Contrasting the same subject matter in three techniques – painting, mosaic, and silver work – makes an interesting study. While the painting has a delightful spontaneity, and the mosaic is lively but not particularly fine, the silver, undoubt-edly made for a wealthy client, shows gorgeous detail in an expensive material.

93 Mildenhall dish, detail of Bacchus and the panther. Silver. Mid-fourth century AD. Diam. of dish: 61 cm (2 ft).

The worship of Roman gods spread throughout the empire, even to the farthest reaches of Roman influence. A statue of Mercury, the god of trade, merchants, and travellers, was found in 1979 in Uley, Gloucestershire, where it came from a temple that was almost certainly dedicated to him (**fig. 94**). The beautiful large head, belonging to an over life-size statue, was carved out of local limestone from the Cotswolds, and is a product of a local sculptor. The god's hair has curls made in a distinctive and idiosyncratic manner undoubtedly characteristic of the artist. The handsome features, and eyes with carved irises, look classical and show that the sculptor was familiar with Roman conventions.

Also from Uley, and associated with the Temple of Mercury, is a curse tablet, one of about 200 found at the site.[3] This lead sheet, about 12 centimetres (5 inches) high, threatens a thief with all sorts of nasty consequences if the stolen item is not returned.[4] It reads:

Biccus gives Mercury whatever he has lost (that the thief), whether man or male [sic] may not urinate nor defecate nor speak nor sleep nor stay awake nor (have) well being or health, unless he bring (it) in the Temple of Mercury. …

94 Head of Mercury. Limestone. From Uley, Gloucestershire. Second century AD. H. 30 cm (11⅝ in).

In other words, unspeakable things will happen to the perpetrator unless the stolen item is returned. Such curse tablets are common, many of them having been found nearby in Bath, the ancient Aquae Sulis.[5] There, the tablets tend to curse people for having stolen clothing while the owner was taking the baths. Quite often curse tablets are found in graves, or in the bottom of a well where they had evidently been thrown.

Imperial cults

While rulers of the Hellenistic Greeks from Alexander the Great onwards had been worshipped as gods, and while Julius Caesar attempted to trace his origin to the goddess Venus, Augustus set precedents that made a pattern for the rest of the imperial period: living emperors were not to be considered divine, but deceased emperors usually were. Yet they were not quite the same as those in the normal pantheon of divinities. Two of the main ways in which an emperor would be associated with a divine cult were to have events, such as his birthday or date of accession to the throne, celebrated by public holidays, feasts and sacrifices, much as one celebrated days dedicated to the gods; and to be deified upon his death.[6] When the latter occurred, an emperor (or his wife) would occasionally be granted a temple as well as priests and days dedicated to celebrations of his divinity. Normally an emperor would not become divine until after his death, but in the East, even living emperors were sometimes worshipped as gods. Maniacal emperors such as Caligula and Commodus demanded divine worship during their lifetimes, and Domitian declared himself *Dominus et Deus* (Lord and God).

Whole buildings would be dedicated to the imperial cult. For instance, at Aphrodisias in Turkey, a shrine called the Sebasteion (Temple to the Revered) is dedicated to Augustus and his Julio-Claudian descendants. In a three-storey structure, sculptured reliefs of the emperors and of divine beings were displayed between the supporting columns. In Baia, on the Bay of Naples, a shrine of the Augustales – the priests who were in charge of the worship of the emperors – incorporated over life-size nude marble statues of the emperors Titus and Vespasian in identical poses. Wealthy freedmen often served as priests for such shrines.

95 Relief of Aeneas, Iulus and the sow with her piglets. Marble. AD 140–50. H. 35.5 cm (14 in).

Mythology

Roman religion was intimately intertwined with mythology, and the two cannot be easily separated. Many Roman myths are related to the founding of cities and thus give a venerable origin to the people who inhabited them. One of the best is the story related in Virgil's *Aeneid* (8.36–48; 8.81–5; 8.388–93). A marble relief (**fig. 95**) tells what happened, starting with the Trojan soldiers at the right, still occupying the ship that brought them to Italian shores. Aeneas, their leader, had been told that when he found a white sow and her thirty piglets, that would indicate where he was to plant his city, Lanuvium. The relief shows Aeneas arriving in Italy, holding the hand of his son Iulus who follows behind him. At the left they come upon a sow and her suckling piglets within a cave. The fertility of the sow suggests by implication that the settlement founded by Aeneas and its inhabitants will grow and prosper. A Roman *sestertius* from the reign of the emperor Antoninus Pius (**fig. 96**) shows the sow and piglets at a tiny scale.[7]

96 The sow and piglets. Brass *sestertius* of Antoninus Pius. Mid-second century AD. Diam. 3 cm (1¼ in), Wt. 23.96 g.

Another mythological tale, this time derived from the Greeks, relates the story of the building of the 'good ship Argo' that brought the hero Jason and the Argonauts to the land of Colchis, where he captured the golden fleece. Here, on a terracotta relief (**fig. 97**), the helmeted goddess Minerva supervises the building of the ship as her owl rests on a pillar behind her and her shield leans against her chair. Tiphys, the helmsman, holds the yard as Argos, the shipbuilder, works on the boat, driving in a nail with a hammer. It is a scene of activity, yet with the quiet and calming influence of Minerva.

Another myth borrowed from the Greeks tells the story of a wild beast that had to be killed. Because the king of Calydon had neglected to honour Diana with a sacrifice, the goddess sent a huge boar to terrorize the land. The king gathered together a band of brave hunters from all over Greece, including Meleager, to try to get rid of the animal. However it was Atalanta, a woman, who first wounded the boar, after which Meleager killed it. Meanwhile, Meleager had fallen in love with Atalanta, and, because she had been the first to draw blood, he gave her the boar skin. However, the men in the hunt did not appreciate this honour being given to a woman, and a fight broke out. Meleager killed his uncles, after which his mother, in revenge, caused Meleager's death by putting a particular burnt branch in the fire. It had been prophesied by the Fates that when that specific piece of wood which she had been keeping safe was consumed, Meleager would die.

97 Relief of Minerva and the Argonauts. Terracotta. First century AD. Said to have been found near Porta Latina. H. 61 cm, W. 53 cm (24 x 21 in).

98 Meleager. Mosaic.
From Halicarnassus.
Fourth century AD.
H. 1.4 m, W. 1.67 m
(4 ft 7 in x 5 ft 5 in).

In another mosaic from Halicarnassus (**fig. 98**), from the same villa as the mosaic of Dionysus and the panther (fig. 92), a variation on the traditional story is depicted. Instead of the boar, a leopard has been substituted. There is no question that this is Meleager because his name is written above in Greek, and the companion piece shows Atalanta. Meleager rides his spirited multicoloured horse as he spears the diminutive spotted leopard. The hero wears a white tunic with round medallion, a grey cape that billows out behind him to emphasize his speed, and boots.

Such mythological scenes could appear in many different contexts, whether decorating homes or temples or public buildings. The stories would be so familiar to the public that they would need no explanation, but local variations in the details were not unheard of.

Temples to the gods

Although gods and goddesses could be worshipped in homes, alongside roadways, and virtually anywhere, they also had formal sanctuaries specifically dedicated to them. Roman towns were endowed with numerous temples to universal as well as local deities. These buildings usually followed a particular form that was ultimately derived from the Etruscans. As seen on the Temple of Portunus[8] in Rome (**fig. 99**), a high platform supported a structure that normally had a porch with columns at the front of the building (see p. 21, fig. 10, also with the high platform and frontal porch). Some temples would have

99 The Temple of Portunus ('Fortuna Virilis'), Rome. Late second century BC.

more than one sanctuary, in which case the platform would be wider. Three doors would lead to three separate *cellae* (or inner chambers) dedicated to different gods, as in the case of the Capitoline Temple in Rome, where Jupiter, Juno and Minerva were worshipped together. A flight of steep stairs led up to the porch, providing the only means of entering the temple itself – in contrast to Greek temples that normally had steps on all four sides.

The decorative motifs of Roman architecture were heavily influenced by Greek prototypes, although sometimes altered to suit Roman taste. The Temple of Portunus is an Ionic temple, with the volutes on the capitals that are the most distinctive feature of this architectural order. Other Roman temples followed the Greek Doric order, sometimes modified to what is known as 'Tuscan'; and Greek Corinthian is commonly found as well (see figs. 10 and 100). A new order, more or less combining Ionic and Corinthian, is called 'Composite', and can be seen on the Arch of Titus (p. 41, fig. 33). The Colosseum (p. 84, fig. 73) in Rome bears the Doric, Ionic and Corinthian orders as decorative features on the exterior.

100 The Pantheon, Rome (exterior). AD 125–8.

The Pantheon in Rome (**fig. 100**) is one of the most extraordinary buildings from antiquity, and one of the greatest buildings ever constructed. Its survival may be credited to the fact that early on it was converted from a pagan temple to a Christian church. It was therefore cared for and its lead roof repaired as necessary. Built under Hadrian, but replacing an earlier building constructed under Augustus, it was dedicated to all the gods, as the Greek word 'pan-theon' indicates.

From the exterior it looks at first glance like a typical Roman temple. Its front porch was on a platform that was approached by a flight of stairs (now buried below the level of the modern pavement). The round 'drum' of the interior and the dome on top are not so obvious from ground level, and would have been even less so in antiquity when a colonnade ran around a large rectangular square in front of the building. An inscription across the front identifies Agrippa, Augustus' friend and son-in-law, as the builder, but in fact Hadrian is giving credit to the patron of the earlier building on this site. The brick stamps can be dated to approximately a ten-year period, *c.* AD 117–27, and the building went up about AD 125–8. These stamps identify the maker of the bricks and give a reference to a consul or other historical marker that allows specific dating of the construction.

Walking through the great bronze doors into the rotunda of the Pantheon is a remarkable experience. Instead of the typical rectangular *cella*, this sanctuary astonishes any viewer by its huge round space capped by an enormous dome with a hole (*oculus*) in the centre of it (**fig. 101**). The grand open area, apparently unsupported by verticals to hold up the dome, is hard to fathom. In fact, the walls of the drum, with their embedded brick arches that give extra strength, are only part of the explanation. The shape of the dome itself is an important part of the construction: the exterior is saucer-shaped with a stepped base, while the interior of the dome is a perfect hemisphere. This combination

101 The Pantheon, Rome (interior).

allows the weight of the dome to be thrust outward upon the walls of the drum at the same time that the downward thrust of the interior dome pushes the weight toward the ground. Other construction features include the square indentations, known as coffering, that help to strengthen the fabric while they lighten the load; and the ingenious composition of the dome, whereby the lower parts are made of a heavy concrete mixture that gets lighter and lighter as it approaches the oculus. Near the top the concrete is made of pumice. The complete and rigid circle of the concrete mass acts as a locking device, rather like the keystone in an arch.

The oculus itself allows light and air into the building, and is the only source of natural light other than the door. The circle of light from the oculus moves perceptibly around the dome and walls over the course of the day, making the observer aware of the movement of the sun. The word *oculus* itself means 'eye', and the opening in fact gives a view onto the sky above, reminding worshippers (and modern visitors) of the cosmic forces. Whatever the weather, it comes inside, whether sun or rain or snow, but it affects only a relatively small portion of the floor area. The marble floor has ancient perforations, and when it rains, the water goes down those holes into the Roman drains that lie beneath the paving. Hardly could there be a more dramatic reminder of the long-lasting skills of Roman engineers.

102 Lamp with Luna in a chariot drawn by bulls. Bronze. H. 18 cm (7 in).

Votive and household religious objects

Votive objects were common in both houses and temples. A bronze leg and a marble relief of a leg dedicated to the health deities Asclepius and Hygieia[9] were objects probably meant to bring healing to the respective donors' legs. Terracotta body parts (including an eye, ear, breast, and internal organs) were similarly intended as offerings to facilitate healing of ailments in those places. Breasts and wombs were gifts that for many women would have been accompanied by prayers for fertility (see p. 136, fig. 142).

Many household objects would have images of gods, either for decoration, or because one hoped the god would somehow be present through the representation. For instance a bronze oil lamp represents Luna, goddess of the moon, in a chariot drawn by two bulls (**fig. 102**). This was a hanging lamp supported by three chains that connected to a ring at the top. Luna is shown as a woman with a crescent moon on her head, driving a chariot across the sky.[10] Her drapery floats behind her in the form of a crescent, appearing like wings that allow her to hover on top of (instead of standing in) her chariot. The two lively bulls prance like horses, drawing her along as she holds the (now lost) reins in her hands. Functioning as an oil lamp, two nozzles for the wicks are placed on the outer sides of the two bulls, and a third is located at the back of Luna's head. The hole for pouring in the oil is in the body of the chariot.

Foreign influences

One of the strengths of the whole Roman system was its willingness to adapt to foreign influences. This included the absorption of the religions of the people they conquered, and the embracing of gods from other cultures. Often the foreign god would be subsumed into a Roman god or goddess who was somewhat akin to the other one.

A bronze statuette represents Silvanus (**fig. 104**), god of uncultivated land. He wears a pine wreath, goat skin, and sandals with leather tops that are folded over, but is otherwise naked; and he holds a branch in his left hand. The Gaulish Sucellus, a Celtic god of agriculture (**fig. 103**), whose beard and features look like Jupiter, is actually often equated with the Roman Silvanus. The bronze

BELOW LEFT 103 Statuette of Sucellus. Bronze. First–third century AD. Said to have been found at Vienne. H. 28 cm (11 in).

BELOW RIGHT 104 Statuette of Sylvanus. Bronze. First–second century AD. From Nocera, Campania. H. 17 cm (6¾ in).

A mithraic boy becomes Paris

When statues were repaired and restored, the sculptor felt at liberty to alter the identity of the figure if he so desired. Such was the case with an ancient marble statue of a boy who was an attendant of Mithras (**fig. 105**). This was one of a pair, each of whom carried a burning torch in his hand. They were found in a grotto near the River Tiber outside Rome. (The other is in the Louvre.) An eighteenth-century sculptor restored the boy as Paris, the Trojan prince who had to choose which of three goddesses was the most beautiful. A competition called 'The Judgment of Paris' was set up between Minerva, Juno and Venus (Athena, Hera, and Aphrodite). Each of the goddesses tried to bribe Paris with something marvellous so that he would choose her. Paris offered the prize, a golden apple, to Venus because the goddess offered him the most beautiful of all women, Helen, as his lover. This led to the Trojan War because after Helen had disappeared from her home and husband to go off with Paris, the Greeks assembled a fleet and sailed to Troy to try and retrieve her.

The mithraic boy was given an apple in one hand instead of the burning torch he had previously carried. This was sufficient to identify him as Paris. He wears a soft headdress known as a Phrygian cap, a tunic, trousers, shoes and cloak. After its restoration, the statue was sold by the dealer Thomas Jenkins to Count Moriz Fries (1777–1826), a collector of art and patron of Beethoven.

105 Statue of Paris, formerly an attendant of Mithras. Marble. H. 1.37 m (4 ft 6 in).

figure carried a hammer or long-handled mallet (now lost) that was to provide protection, and that refers to his name, literally 'the good striker'. Sucellus wears a short Gallic tunic with a fringed border and a wolf skin over his head. Such gods of the field and woods appealed especially to rural folk and were popular all over the Roman world.

As the Romans spread to the East, they adopted gods from foreign lands in that part of the world as well. One of these was Mithras (**fig. 106**), a god first taken over from Mesopotamia by the Hellenistic Greeks. He originated as a Persian god of the sun. The cult was limited to male initiates, and because of its secret nature, not many of its rites were recorded. The god killed a bull by slitting its throat (the *tauroctony*), and the blood was preserved for drinking by the initiates who believed that it caused regeneration. In the statue, Mithras kneels on the bull and holds its mouth open as he plunges the knife into its back. The statue is reminiscent of Victory slaying a bull, seen above (p. 42, fig. 34). Mithras' dog licks the wound where blood spurts out and a snake slithers up to the wound. A scorpion is clawing the bull's testicles. Mithras wears a Phrygian cap, emphasizing his origin in Anatolia or the Near East. The head of the god has a beautiful classical face without much expression, but it is a copy made in modern times.

Mithraic initiates would gather in artificial underground chapels that were often reminiscent of caves. They seem to have been dark, dank places. Evidence survives for various lighting effects that must have augmented the impression of mystery for those attending the rituals.[11] After the initiation, men would rise through seven ranks, each associated with an animal or god – such as a raven, a lion, or Saturn. The highest level was the father, but lower ranks also had authority within the religious hierarchy.

Sometimes information about the Mithraic religion can be gleaned from objects found with related text or symbolism. A bronze tablet[12] probably from Ostia is dedicated to Sextus Pompeius Maximus, chief priest of the cult of Mithras and president of the guild of ferrymen. On the top of the tablet is a bust of Mithras crowned by solar rays. A sacrificial knife and patera (offering bowl) are placed at the sides of the bust. Maximus is known from another text to have restored a sanctuary of Mithras at Ostia

106 Mithras and the bull. Marble. Second century AD. From Rome. H. 1.29 m, L. 1.47 m (4 ft 3 in x 4 ft 10 in).

107 Relief of the moon god, Mên. Marble. Late second century AD. H. 41 cm, W. 25.5 cm (16 in x 10 in).

Other eastern gods were assimilated by the Romans, including Mên, the Anatolian moon god. He appears in a marble relief (**fig. 107**) standing on a small bull, its head drooping over the edge and its body sprawled awkwardly at his feet. Mên carries a staff and fruit, and wears a Phrygian cap. The two ends of a crescent moon – his main attribute – curl behind his shoulders. He was believed to have healing powers, for which the person who dedicated this relief, Agathopous, offers his thanks. Mên was closely allied with Attis, consort of the Great Mother goddess, Cybele, except that he specifically brought control of the night to Attis' other attributes.[13] Attis is the subject of a lamp[14] that shows him in a cult car pulled by four rams.

Another of the major religions to come from abroad, this time from Egypt, is the cult of Isis. The Egyptian goddess of childbirth and fertility, she became extremely important in the Roman pantheon, and was often associated with Aphrodite, as well as (at one time or another) Diana, Minerva, Demeter, and the Mother Goddess.[15] A marble statue of Isis (**fig. 109**) was made in Italy, *c.* 120–50 AD, and was bought by the notable eighteenth century collector Charles Townley. The piece had been broken at the right wrist, and was incorrectly repaired by a restorer, who showed her carrying fruit; originally she held a *sistrum*, or rattle, in her right hand.[16] In her other hand she carried a *situla*, or bucket, that was filled with water from the Nile. Two snakes, symbol of Isis, with the disc of the moon between them, adorn her headdress. Temples to Isis sprang up in many Roman cities; the one in Pompeii had already been found in the eighteenth century.

Jupiter was often assimilated with other gods, especially with those from Egypt. Two examples of this are Jupiter Ammon (affiliated with the Egyptian Amun) and Jupiter Serapis, whose marble head is shown with a heavy beard and long hair, some of which falls on his forehead (**fig. 108**).[17] Serapis wears a distinctive hat, the *kalathos* decorated with olive branches, a headdress associated with the god. His face was originally tinted red. Townley wrote, 'Unfortunately upon its discovery it fell into the hands of Francesco Cavaceppi, an ignorant sculptor, who used every means to expunge the red colour by the spirit of salt and aquafortis [acid], but the ancient tint is still visible.'[18] A temple to Serapis is recorded in York in an inscription from the late second or early third century AD.[19]

Among the other foreign religious groups that were active under Roman rule were the Jews. One of many objects to survive from Jewish homes or places of worship is an oil lamp with a stylized menorah decorating the top.[20] Jewish communities sprang up in many cities, and some held distinguished places in

108 Head and bust of Jupiter
Serapis. Marble. H. 45.7 cm
(1 ft 6 in).

109 Statue of Isis. Marble.
H. 1.27 m (4 ft 2 in).

110 The Synagogue at Sardis, Turkey. Fifth century AD in the view seen here.

111 Floor mosaic from Hinton St Mary, Dorset. Fourth century AD. L. 8.1 m, W. 5.2 m (26 ft 6 in x 17 ft).

the civic center of town. For example the synagogue at Sardis in western Turkey (**fig. 110**) was incorporated into the Roman gymnasium complex, and in fact was one of the largest structures within it.[21] It had probably been converted from a space designed for use as an administrative centre. The long, narrow building, with an apse at one end and shrines for the Torah and other sacred texts at the other, occupied one whole side of the large palaestra, or exercise field, in front of the gymnasium. Carved reliefs on the walls and floor mosaics decorated the interior, and fragments of a large marble menorah were found within it. A forecourt with a fountain stood in front of the building. Flanking the synagogue on the other side from the palaestra, at least in Byzantine times, was a row of shops.[22] Thus, the main Jewish sanctuary was nestled between a huge athletic complex that included baths and a large entrance court, and a commercial street lined with shops. It testifies to the prominence of the Jewish community in the Roman city. And from here we may extrapolate a much larger point, namely that foreign religions took a firm foothold in Roman life and were widely tolerated by the authorities while enthusiastically embraced by the populace. The Roman authorities in fact required only observance of the imperial cult, which considered the deceased members of the imperial families as a divine group owed religious allegiance by all. That was the principal difficulty for Jews and Christians: they believed in one true God and could not just add another to please the Roman government.

112 The Projecta
Casket, from the
Esquiline Treasure,
Rome. *c.* AD 380.
H. 28 cm, L. 55 cm
(11 x 21½ in).

After the Edict of Milan (AD 313) that declared tolerance for all religions, it may have seemed safer for Christians to use more specific imagery and inscriptions than had previously been possible. They often maintained some pagan forms at the same time that they began to include Christian symbolism. A fourth-century floor mosaic from Hinton St Mary, Dorset (**fig. 111**), found in 1963, bears a medallion with the mythological hero Bellerophon riding his winged horse Pegasus, spearing the monster Chimaera. This mosaic, in a small room, was balanced in the adjoining larger room by another central medallion, this time with Christ's head set against the Christogram (the Greek letters chi and rho, the first two letters of Christ's name). This is the earliest known image of Christ in Britain. The owners of the villa were betwixt and between classical mythology and Christian beliefs. Traditional mythological motifs such as the four heads in the corners of the larger room may represent the four winds, often seen in pagan imagery, or they may represent the four Evangelists.

Similarly, a magnificent silver box known as the Projecta Casket (**fig. 112**), found on the Esquiline Hill in Rome, also displays the mixture of Christian and pagan traditions in the late fourth century AD. A decidedly Christian inscription marks the box that was probably a wedding gift for the marriage of Projecta (a Christian) and Secundus (a pagan). It wishes for the good life for this pair under Christ: SECVNDE ET PROIECTA VIVATIS IN CHRI[STO]. Yet, in the classical spirit, many scenes from the traditional pagan repertory decorate the box. On one side panel of the lid, Venus admires herself in a mirror while surrounded by cupids riding on human-headed hippocamps, those hybrids of a human, horse and sea-serpent. Thus, the two traditions endure side by side.

7

The Household

The structures and objects found at Pompeii and Herculaneum offer a picture of daily life that is unparalleled elsewhere in the ancient world (**fig. 113**). The two cities were re-discovered in the mid-eighteenth century; buried under the ash of Mount Vesuvius were the streets, shops, and houses of rich and poor, indiscriminately destroyed on that fateful August day in AD 79. Some of the people were not able to get away from the deadly fumes and falling ash, and they were buried along with their belongings. In 1863 a remarkable technique for revealing these final moments was devised by Giuseppe Fiorelli, director of the excavations at Pompeii. He poured liquid plaster into some holes that he and his colleagues were finding. The plaster filled the voids made by the bodies that had long since disintegrated, but their shape had been preserved in the now stone-hard ash. Then when the ash was removed and the plaster itself was excavated, it revealed the dead and dying bodies in three-dimensional form. In one case a pet dog, who had been chained up, was found.

113 View of Herculaneum and Mt Vesuvius.

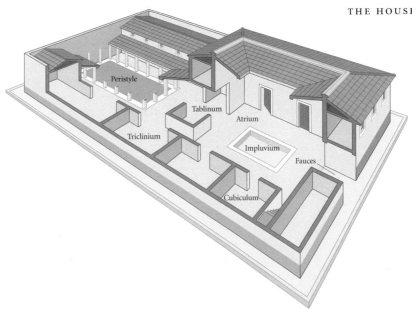

114 Drawing of a patrician Roman house.

115 Atrium in the House of the Silver Wedding, Pompeii. Mid-first century BC.

116 Lion-head water spout. Terracotta. H. 15 cm (6 in).

117 Peristyle, House of the Vettii, Pompeii. Mid-first century AD.

Many of the wealthy lived in grand houses that usually had a long, narrow configuration to the plan, with an inward looking orientation (**fig. 114**). Instead of windows opening out onto the street, a wall enclosed both the living area and the garden behind. The family living in such houses consisted not only of blood relatives, but also slaves, servants, and tutors for the children.

Entering the house, one passed through a narrow hallway called the vestibule, or *fauces* (literally, 'throat'). This opened into a large roofed court or atrium, in the centre of which was a rectangular pool, the *impluvium* (**fig. 115**). In the roof above, a central opening, the *compluvium*, let in light, air and rain. The roof sloped inward toward this central opening where terracotta water spouts in the shape of the foreparts of animals (**fig. 116**) guided the streams of water that landed in the pool below. The rather doglike lion-head spout shown here is one of the more common types, and has been found often in the region of Rome and Latium as well as Pompeii. Its origins can be traced back to South Italy and to mainland Greece, where lion-head spouts in marble, but without the forelegs, were widespread. Here the water poured out between the legs, whereas in Greek models it flowed through the animal's mouth.

Off the atrium were small rooms ranging from bedrooms (*cubicula*) to the dining room (*triclinium*). The word *triclinium* (three benches) was taken over by the Romans from the Greek word for the arrangement of three couches set around a rectangular space for dining. This was standard at symposia (drinking parties) and dinner parties. Looking straight through the central axis, one

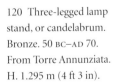

118 Fountain jet with dolphin. Bronze. From Constantinople. Second–third century AD. H. 23.5 cm, L. 30.5 cm (9¼ in x 12 in).

119 Window pane. Opaque bluish-green glass. From near Herculaneum. *c.* AD 1–70. Thickness 3 mm (⅛ in).

120 Three-legged lamp stand, or candelabrum. Bronze. 50 BC–AD 70. From Torre Annunziata. H. 1.295 m (4 ft 3 in).

caught a glimpse of the peristyle behind (**fig. 117**), an enclosed garden with columns around the periphery and often rooms beyond the colonnade. Within the garden, fountains played near the bushes and flowers. A fountain spout shows how these worked: a dolphin still has the remains of a tube for water in its mouth (**fig. 118**). The bushes and trees that have been planted here are the same varieties as those in the ancient gardens. Archaeologists have been able to determine the species of the plants by pouring plaster into the root systems that had rotted away, leaving cavities, just as the human bodies had done. By studying those roots, the specific plants could be identified and then replaced.

Glass windows existed in wealthier homes, and would often be set between the interior parts of the house and the garden area. Typically, the window panes were translucent, but not transparent (**fig. 119**), as this one from near Herculaneum indicates. Natural light came into the house through the *compluvium* and through openings onto the peristyle, but in addition, and for night time, oil lamps lit the interior (see p. 83, fig. 72). Candelabra, three-legged supports often ending in lions' feet or hooves (**fig. 120**), held the lamps at a certain height so that their light could have the maximum effect.

A pile of lamps

121 A pile of lamps. Clay. Found in a tower of the city wall of Ephesus, Turkey. AD 50–120. H. 14 cm, W. 11 cm (5½ x 4½ in).

When pottery is fired, each piece has to be separated from every other one, or else they may stick to each other and be ruined. That is a risk when a kiln gets much too hot, which is probably what happened to a pile of lamps in the kiln (**fig. 121**). They fused to each other and were deformed; now only the decoration on the top one is visible: a lap dog lying on a couch. There were nine lamps in all.

Lamps were generally made in two moulds, one for the upper half and one for the lower. The clay would be pressed into the mould, and allowed to dry somewhat so that the clay would shrink. Then the hollow form could easily be extracted; the two halves would be joined together and fired in the kiln. Many moulds are not fine, and the workmanship tends to be a bit rough. But exceptions can be found, where lamps are carefully made, as in the case of the gladiator scene (fig. 72). Bronze lamps tend to be much finer, and can be both elaborate and elegant.

Every lamp has to have at least two holes: one for the wick and one for filling the lamp with oil as well as allowing the air to flow through. Most lamps have two holes for the air, and some have more than one wick. The oil used was usually olive oil although castor and linseed oil were also known. Some lamps were hung from chains, while others would sit on a ledge or on a candelabrum – a candle or lamp holder (see fig. 120).

Somewhere near the entrance to the house would hang a *tintinnabulum* (**fig. 122**) – an onomatopoeic word that mimics the sound of the bells that hang on small chains from the object. This was an apotropaic bronze, intended to bring good luck (or literally, 'turning away evil'), made up of phalluses that were thought to protect the house and its inhabitants. It was also believed that it would bring prosperity to the family. This particular *tintinnabulum* is constructed of a lion's body and hind legs, but the forepart of the animal is, instead, a single large winged penis. In addition, the tail is a phallus, and the lion's penis is hugely oversized. Bells hang from the main tip, the wings, the penis, and one of the legs. It is unrecorded as to whether men and women looked upon such items in different ways. The protective power of the phallus was also used in the form of rings for men, women and even children, who sometimes wore a tiny ring with a phallus on it.[1] The image also was carved on plaques that decorated the exterior of a house or a street corner.

122 Tintinnabulum.
Bronze. First century AD.
H. 13.5 cm (5¼ in).

123 Lararium in the House
of the Vettii, Pompeii.
AD 63–79.

Protecting the house as well were the Lares, or household gods, who were often represented by small statuettes that were worshipped on a daily basis. A bronze Lar (**fig. 124**) has holes at the pupils of the eyes where an inlay would have been inserted. He carries a libation bowl and a drinking horn whose lower end takes the shape of a dolphin. He prances around on tip-toe, wearing boots and what looks like a short swirly skirt. Actually it was a way of tucking up the toga, known as *cinctus Gabinus*, that offered greater freedom of movement than the traditional fall of the toga. It was also required dress for certain types of sacrifice (Livy 5.46.2). Sometimes the Lares are shown together with the 'genius' of the house, as seen in the painting in the *lararium* ('shrine of the Lares') in the House of the Vettii at Pompeii (**fig. 123**). The face of the genius (something like a 'spirit') is a portrait of the owner of the house, who is sacrificing by pouring a liquid offering onto the ground. The Lares each hold a drinking horn above their heads with one hand and pour the liquid into a little bucket

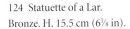

124 Statuette of a Lar.
Bronze. H. 15.5 cm (6⅛ in).

held by the other hand. Usually a snake or two, symbols of underworld gods, slither along towards an altar to enjoy the offerings set out for them.

Another belief common among the Romans was that the Penates guarded their homes. These minor gods were originally thought to protect the storerooms, but eventually came to look after the whole household. Penates also protected the state. The most celebrated story in this regard is that Aeneas carried the Penates from Troy and set them up in his new cities in Italy, thus carrying the protection with him.

Women in the home

The role of women in Roman society was based largely on their position as wife and mother. In the public sphere, even though they could not vote or officially take part in public life, many of them had a big influence not only on their men folk directly, but also through them on politics and history. Livia, the wife of Augustus, the first emperor, is a good example. She frequently interfered in political affairs through her husband and ultimately engineered the accession of her son to the imperial throne. Nero's mother, Agrippina the Younger, engaged in several intrigues to ensure Nero's succession, as we learn from Tacitus (especially *Annales* Books 12 and 25).

Marriage was a major event in the lives of Roman women, when they normally left their own family to become part of the husband's extended household. Roman law provided for several rites for the marriage ceremony, depending upon the relative status of the people involved. In addition, various similar social customs were observed, whatever the precise details of the formalities. These included ritual washing and the cutting of the girl's hair to signify her new status. A new style of dress was required as well, declaring the young woman's married state to all. The bride, often very young, would dedicate her girlish clothes and her toys to the Lares or to Venus, as she donned her new outfit.

A large fragment of a sarcophagus made of bluish Greek marble (**fig. 125**) shows the joining of right hands, *dextrarum iunctio*, between the man and

125 Marriage sarcophagus. Marble. Townley bought the piece from the sculptor Carlo Albacini. H. 98.4 cm, W. 78 cm (3 ft 2¾ in x 2 ft 6¾ in).

ABOVE 126 Scent bottle in the shape of a boot. Terracotta. Late first or early second century AD. Perhaps made in Cnidos. H. 12.7 cm (5 in).

ABOVE RIGHT 127 Shoe leather. From Antinöopolis, Egypt. L. 27 cm (10½ in).

the woman.[2] This gesture, a part of the marriage ceremony, was often depicted in Roman art, especially on sarcophagi. It would have been followed by a sacrifice to Jupiter. In the relief the man wears a toga and is shown holding a scroll, probably the marriage document itself, in his left hand. The woman, turned toward the front, wears a clinging Greek garment, a chiton, and a cloak draped over her head and shoulders. Both wear sandals. Behind them is a woman, the *pronuba*, who drapes her arms over both figures. She is a married woman, the maid of honour, who looks after the detailed arrangements for the wedding. She also represents Juno Pronuba, goddess of marriage; and at least symbolically, she leads the bride to the marriage bed. A man stands at the left, and a female attendant (whose left hand is all that remains) at the right. A boy, Hymenaeus (god of marriage ceremonies), would have stood in the centre between the couple, and he would have held a flaming torch, the tip of which can be seen in front of the bride's right thigh. This represents the most traditional and formal wedding ceremony, the union of two citizens of equal station.

Many objects from the women's sphere were found in the houses of Pompeii and Herculaneum, as well as in Egypt, and are often of perishable materials. One such mundane item, from Egypt, is the black and tan leather slip-on shoe with stitching and trim in contrasting colours (**fig. 127**). Another is a terracotta scent bottle in the shape of a boot, laced up the front (**fig. 126**). The boot has hobnails indicated on the bottom, placed to form an alpha and omega, as well as the design of a swastika. The collocation of alpha and omega must indicate that the owner and possibly the maker was a Christian, making a sly iconographical reference to the words of Jesus in *Revelation* I.8: 'I am the Alpha and Omega'. The two letters are partly hidden by the swastika, which was a widely used symbol, often representing the sun, in many cultures going back to Neolithic times.

128 Comb of
Modestina. Ivory.
Probably third or
fourth century AD.
L. 12.7 cm (5 in).

Other items used by women include bronze needles, a bone pin carved with the head of a woman, and a double-sided ivory comb (**fig. 128**) inscribed in delicate openwork with the name MODESTINA, followed by VAEE, letters that probably stand for a 'virtuous, excellent, and admirable wife' (Vxor Admiranda et Egregia).[3] Much jewellery for women has been found all over the Roman world. A necklace in gold with lovely lavender-coloured amethysts (**fig. 129**) is a good example of a treasure of a wealthy lady, and many such items are recorded in painting or sculpture (see figs. 143 and 180).

A completely different kind of item, a bronze tag (**fig. 130**) may be the remains of something worn by a slave – if not by a dog. It says: *Tene me ne fugia et revoca me ad domumnum [sic] evviventium in ara callisti.* That seems to be a rather uneducated Latin message, to be roughly interpreted as 'Hold me, lest I flee, and return me to my master Viventius on the estate of Callistus.' A loop at the top is now broken away, but would have been used to hold the tag around the neck with a chain.

129 Necklace with
amethysts. Third
century AD.

130 Slave tag or dog tag.
Bronze. Fourth century AD.
Diam. 5.7 cm (2¼ in).

Children

It was important for a child to be recognized by its father in order to be considered a citizen and full member of the family, and eligible to share in the family estate. In the case of a boy, it affected whether he would become Pater Familias, or the overall head of the household, who controlled the destiny of wife, children, unrelated supporters, and slaves. The father would lift the child ('lifting' was the technical term), and in doing so, accept him or her as his own, due all the rights that such a relationship would eventually entail.

The day-to-day care of young children was normally entrusted to female slaves as wet-nurse or nanny, and perhaps eventually to a tutor, usually a man. Both sexes were educated at least to a secondary level, and occasionally one hears of a girl who has distinguished herself as a physician or in some other profession. Certainly we have evidence for literate wives of military commanders in the fragments of letters from Vindolanda, the fort in northern England (see chapter 2). A particularly telling example is a letter from the wife of a commander to a friend, actually addressed as 'sister', at a different camp, inviting her to a birthday party (p. 48, fig. 43).[4]

In wealthier households, an educated slave, often a Greek, would be the tutor who taught the children right in their own home. Children learned to write by inscribing their letters on writing tablets covered with wax (**fig. 131**), and adults used such tablets as well. The one shown here, with four leaves of a wooden tablet, is from Egypt, where such items in perishable materials tend to survive well. Papyrus, usually from Egypt, was another material on which people wrote. Papyrus is a reed that grows in marshy conditions, particularly at the edge of the Nile. Its fibrous stem is cut lengthwise, hammered, and then woven to make a strong, durable material. Our word 'paper' derives from papyrus, although the material and texture are different. An example of papyrus on loan to the British Museum preserves a line from Virgil's *Aeneid* that has been repeated seven times as an exercise.[5]

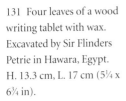

131 Four leaves of a wood writing tablet with wax. Excavated by Sir Flinders Petrie in Hawara, Egypt. H. 13.3 cm, L. 17 cm (5¼ x 6¾ in).

There was plenty of time for childhood pastimes, as many finds all around the empire attest. Circumstances of preservation skew the lists heavily in favour of terracotta dolls or other durable playthings, even from places that favour the preservation of organic materials. Needed are either a dry climate like that of Egypt, where hardly any interaction of air and moisture take place; or else a wet situation where lack of air prevents that same interaction. One of these toys from Egypt is the delightful and lively lead model of a camel (**fig. 133**) who is running with his head stretched forward in a realistic way. Occasionally a piece in more perishable materials survives, like the bone doll from Ephesus (**fig. 132**) that had moving arms and legs – now missing. Her hair is piled up on top of her head and she wears a crown rather like some of the portraits of Sabina, the wife of Hadrian. Her pubic area has been emphasized but not her breasts.

In addition to toys, special tableware and furniture were made for children, or for miniature dedications. Household objects would include items for the baby, such as a terracotta baby feeder with a spout, decorated with a dramatic mask depicting the face of a hairy satyr (**fig. 134**).[6] Small holes at the upper end of the feeder would prevent spillage as the baby drank from the bottom hole.

Games of all kinds were popular throughout the Roman world. Dice made out of bone, stone, or rock crystal were common,[7] and could be very large, such as a facetted green stone marked with Roman numerals.[8] An intriguing eighteenth century analysis of Roman dice is recorded in a footnote by one of the Rymsdyk brothers who illustrated and wrote the text in the first compendium of the British Museum's contents, *Museum Britannicum*, in 1778:

*Dice: Many of these Dice, like other antiquities, are found in various parts of the bowels of the earth, and were lost or dropped by the soldiers, etc. who served under different monarchs … While I was busy in designing

132 Doll, formerly with movable arms and legs, now missing. Bone. From Ephesus. Preserved H. 10 cm (4 in).

BELOW 133 Toy model of a camel. Lead. First century AD. Excavated in Lower Egypt. H. 6 cm, W. 7.5 cm (2 x 3 in), L. 7.5 cm (3 in).

BELOW RIGHT 134 Baby feeder with mask of a satyr. Clay. L. 17 cm (6½ in).

[drawing] these ancient Dice, and turning them with attention, that which struck me most was the disposition of their numbers, i.e. the fortunate and unfortunate chance, are always disposed opposite to each other; suppose six is cast, one will be at the bottom, and if you count the top and bottom together, it will always make seven. ... We have this further remark on Dice, which is: that they should be a true square, and all the angles cut as keen as possible, and the numbers disposed according to the above plan of seven.[9]

Gaming (or gambling) pieces, typically made of bone or ivory, have amusing identifications on them: *Male [E]st* ['bad luck']; *VICTOR*; and *Nugator* ['trifler'].[10] Even board games survive, such as a stone slab with nine inscribed depressions.[11] Quite often on the doorsteps or floors of temples or other public buildings, game boards have been scratched in, affording a place for people to play while they waited for an appointment or for a performance to begin.

Food, diet and the kitchen

When reconstructing the daily lives of the Romans, one must be aware of the difference between the physical remains found in houses and towns, and the textual evidence found in literary descriptions. Ancient authors do not often describe everyday objects nor how they were used, although there are exceptions. The satirical and farcical description of a lavish and almost unimaginable dinner hosted by the super-rich freedman, Trimalchio, was told in Petronius' *Satyricon*. One quickly gets a sense of the extravagance of the meal:

The course that followed our applause failed, however, to measure up to our expectations of our host, but it was so unusual that it took everybody's attention. Spaced around a circular tray were the twelve signs of the zodiac, and over each sign the chef had put the most appropriate food. Thus, over the sign of Aries were chickpeas, over Taurus a slice of beef, a pair of testicles and kidneys over Gemini, a wreath of flowers over Cancer, over Leo an African fig, virgin sowbelly on Virgo, over Libra a pair of scales with a tartlet in one pan and a cheesecake in the other, over Scorpio a crawfish, a lobster on Capricorn, on Aquarius a goose, and two mullets over the sign of the Fishes. The centerpiece was a clod of turf with the grass still green on top and the whole thing surmounted by a fat honeycomb. ... Suddenly the orchestra gave another flourish and four slaves came dancing in and whisked off the top of the tray. Underneath, in still another tray, lay fat capons and sowbellies and a hare tricked out with wings to look like a little Pegasus. At the corners of the tray stood four little gravy boats, all shaped like the satyr Marsyas, with phalluses for spouts and a spicy hot gravy dripping down over several large fish swimming about in the lagoon of the tray.[12]

Elaborate meals like that, if not so fanciful, were served in the homes of the wealthiest citizens on silver plates and platters. Although rare, finds of this sort are incredibly rich. One of these is the Chaourse Hoard consisting of thirty-nine pieces of silver found in France in 1883. Among the objects are 10 cups, a fluted bowl in which to wash one's hands, a large serving dish with a swastika in the middle, and a plate with Mercury in the centre.[13]

In the past more attention has been paid to the richer collections found in imperial palaces and villas, but today an emphasis is placed on the kinds of household objects dug up in excavations, items that range from relief-decorated pottery vessels to iron or bone sewing needles to dice and board games. In this regard, the complete objects retrieved from Pompeii and Herculaneum have provided models to allow a better understanding of the scraps of household objects usually found in excavations.

Bowls are found frequently. They could serve as drinking cups or serving dishes for soup or stew, or containers of nuts and olives. Mould-made examples with relief decoration came mostly from Gaul (modern France), but also from Italy. There they are called Arretine after the city of Arretium, modern Arezzo, where the technique was invented. Often the cheap versions in clay seem to imitate more valuable and elaborately decorated silver vessels.

135 Samian jar with a running dog. Clay. Second century AD. From Felixstowe, Suffolk. H. 18.5 cm (7¼ in).

The so-called Samian jar with running dogs (**fig. 135**) is a fine example of a reddish clay pot that shows a high gloss, perhaps to imitate metalwork. (The name 'Samian' is a misperception based on an earlier opinion that such bowls were made on the island of Samos.)[14] This particular piece is decorated freehand by the 'barbotine' technique, where a thick trail of slip is squeezed out from the narrow end of a bag as if a confectioner were icing a cake. Some of the slip has fallen off, where the join to the pot was not firm enough. This is like the problem mentioned earlier in regard to a clay jar from Colchester (p. 91, fig. 81). The result is much more fluid than designs that are pressed into a mould. The British Museum has on display several moulds for other Samian bowls, as well as for lamps. Often they, like the Arretine wares, are stamped with the name of the factory owner.[15]

136 Edible Fish. Floor
mosaic. *c.* AD 100.
H. 1.04 m, W. 89 cm
(3 ft 5 in x 2 ft 11 in).

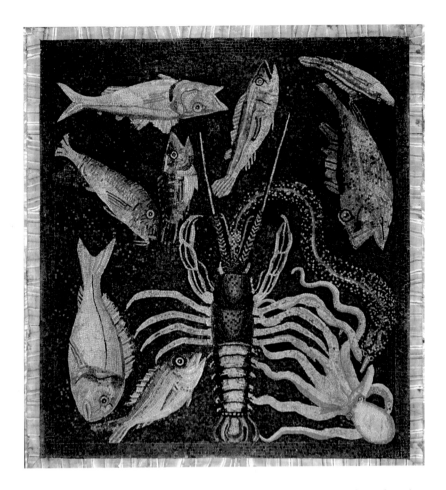

Considerable numbers of *thermopolia* or hot-snack bars have been found at
street corners in Pompeii and at Herculaneum. They must have served a quick
cup of warm soup or wine if not a small mouthful or snack for the general
public as they went about their daily business. This pattern of fast food is
repeated elsewhere around the Roman empire, particularly at Ostia, where
tureens and craters for serving this kind of food have been excavated. This is in
contrast to descriptions of formal dining where the guests recline on couches
that are recorded in several literary works, most prominently by Petronius in
The Satyricon.

In modern archaeology, traces of food stuffs are carefully preserved from
the insides of pots and dishes, and seeds are retrieved by a flotation method
that allows specialists to determine what was being grown and eaten in the
region. Understanding of food and diet can also be gained from wall paintings
and mosaics. The ancient Campanian diet was much like the modern one,
with wine, cereal, and many varieties of seafood. A mosaic (**fig. 136**) that
probably was set in the floor of a triclinium depicts many tasty fish, including

137 'Empress' pepper pot from the Hoxne hoard. Hollow-cast silver, partly gilded. From Hoxne, Suffolk. Buried in the fifth century AD. H. 10.3 cm (4⅛ in).

octopus, spiny lobster, red mullet, and moray eel, all species mentioned by ancient authors. Other fish pictured here are dentex, gilt-head bream, common bass, comber, green wrasse, rainbow wrasse, and scorpion fish. A mosaic such as this would have indicated to guests that the supply of fish in this house was plentiful, even if some of the varieties had to be imported at great expense.

The Greeks had developed a particular ceramic form, known as the fish plate, for such meals, where the profile sloped down to a circular reservoir in the middle for catching the sauce that drained from the fish. This shape would also be a perfectly good place to put the garum sauce as well. Garlic or dill and any number of other herbs and spices might have given added flavour. Fishponds, or *piscinae*, were not infrequent in the wealthier homes, and the emperor Tiberius even had ponds for freshwater and saltwater fish alongside each other at his villa south of Rome at Sperlonga.[16]

A number of rich deposits of silver from the Roman period have been found in Britain. One of the most spectacular, the Hoxne hoard discovered only in 1992, consisted of a huge number of coins (nearly 15,000; see fig. 62 and frontispiece), as well as 200 gold and silver objects from the early fifth century AD. One of the most elaborate pieces is a silver pepper pot (**fig. 137**) in the form of the head and bust of a crowned woman, thought to represent an empress. Various parts are gilded, including the borders of her sleeves, her bracelets and necklaces, her hair, eyes, mouth, and the scroll that she holds in her left hand. A *piperatorium*, as it was called, was made for the expensive spice, pepper, that was imported from India. The hollow silver piece has a disc on the underside that may be turned for filling or sprinkling the pepper, or closed when not in use. The piece, which is set up on short legs, is one of four pepper pots in the Hoxne hoard.

Also among the finds in the Hoxne treasure were numerous spoons, many of which again were gilded (**fig. 138**). A group of nineteen related spoons in a set have similar designs, including hippocamps and other sea creatures in the bowl of the spoon. The group consists of eleven long-handled spoons, six with bird-head handles, and two with dolphin-head handles and perforations in the bowl of the spoon. This treasure seems to have been buried in the hope that the family would some day return to retrieve their objects, but unfortunately for them, that never happened.

138 Spoons from the Hoxne Hoard. Silver. From Hoxne, Suffolk. Buried in the fifth century AD. L. longer spoons: *c.* 13.5 cm (5¼ in).

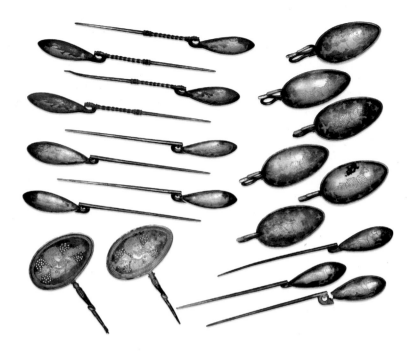

In contrast to those rich objects, kitchen items, such as a bronze food strainer, a frying pan and a baking pan,[17] have been found in abundance in villas around Mt Vesuvius and in Egypt. Sometimes scholars have attempted to create an explanation of how objects of daily life were used by extrapolating from expensive, luxury objects, but more recently greater emphasis has been placed on the cheaper products used in ordinary homes. A remarkably mundane piece seems to sum up the daily life of ordinary Romans: a scrubbing brush (**fig. 139**) with bristles and a wooden handle. Found in Egypt, this could have come out of any modern kitchen.

139 Scrubbing brush. Wooden handle with bristles. From Sedment el Gebel (near Heracleopolis), Egypt. L. 15.5 cm (6¼ in).

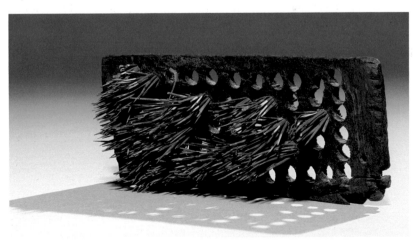

Health, Death and the Afterlife

Healthcare under the Romans could be surprisingly unsophisticated, according to the ancient writings of Pliny the Elder (*Natural History* 29.6–8), and there seems to have been no requirement for the licensing of doctors or the regulation of medicines. Indeed, Pliny tells us that many doctors were known for their wealth rather than their training or medical accomplishments. Disease was usually treated by men who had studied Greek medicine, and often they were themselves Greek. Many were slaves or freedmen, and Julius Caesar enticed Greek doctors to settle in Rome by offering them citizenship.

A gravestone is identified by its Greek inscription as being that of an Athenian doctor called Jason (**fig. 140**). It shows him as an elderly man sitting on a pillow on a folding stool. Dressed in Greek clothing, he is examining a naked boy, with distended belly, who looks at the doctor expectantly. At the right, what appears to be an oversized cupping vessel – used to draw blood – rests on the floor. This remedy was typically used for inflammations. Very hot water was put in the vessel, usually made of glass, and then poured out; then the mouth of the cup was put on the sore or opening, and as it cooled, the vacuum that was created drew out the blood. Even though the piece was found in Athens, and represents a Greek man, nevertheless it was made during the Roman period (second century AD) and shows how Greek culture, learning and medicine continued to hold sway under Roman rule.[1]

Cures for ailments were often associated with bathing, and medical writers recommended taking the baths, or else avoiding them, depending on the problem at hand. Galen, a doctor from the second century AD who came from Pergamum in Asia Minor, wrote extensive medical tracts, frequently talking about bathing as a cure, and Pliny the Younger's letters talk about a sick man who dreams about going to the baths.[2]

To judge by the range of surgical instruments preserved at Pompeii and Herculaneum in particular, the equipment used in medicine was quite advanced. All sorts of treatments were available for the wealthy and the well-connected, but the poor had to rely on faith and patience along with a few traditional herbal remedies. Within a set of mundane instruments, a surgeon's bronze rectal speculum or dilator (**fig. 141**) that worked like forceps stands as

134

140 Tombstone of an Athenian doctor called Jason. Marble. Second century AD. From Athens. H. 79 cm, W. 56 cm (2 ft 7 in x 1 ft 10 in).

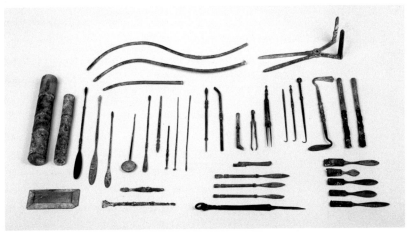

141 Medical instruments, including rectal speculum in the upper right corner. Bronze. First century AD. Said to have been excavated in Italy. L. 9.5 cm (3¾ in).

135

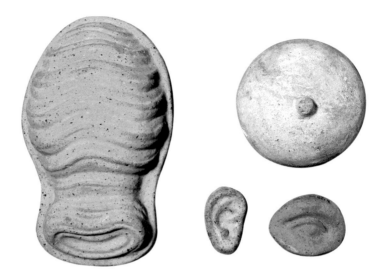

142 Body parts to be offered to the gods. Terracotta. Third–first centuries BC. Womb: 18 cm (7 in), breast, ear and eye.

testimony to the efforts to investigate medical problems in ways that seem remarkably modern. On the other hand, terracotta body parts (**fig. 142**) were used in a superstitious manner, where a person with something wrong would offer the appropriate organ to the gods, hoping for help in the healing of that part of the body. Seen here are a womb, an ear, an eye and a breast. Intestines are also found. Thanks for a cure might also be the motivation for this kind of dedication of body parts (normally in a cheap material).

Much of the material surviving from the Roman era is concerned with death and burial. Whether the burial customs in a particular family were to use cremation or inhumation, both of which could be found commonly after the early second century AD, the dead would be honoured and provided for in the best manner that the relatives could afford. Many containers for ashes or coffins for the bodies have been found, as well as inscriptions on gravestones describing the life and achievements of the deceased. Objects of daily life are also frequently found in tombs and burials because of the belief that the deceased might need such things in the life hereafter. This practice goes back to prehistoric times and is common. A typical grave might hold military paraphernalia for men, bowls and cooking equipment or jewellery for women, or in the case of a child, a doll or toy.

Roman tombs and cemeteries lined the roads outside the walls of towns and cities. This practice was based on the ancient custom of keeping the remains and spirits of the dead away from the living. In Rome, even today, one can see the ancient tombs lining the Via Appia that leads to the south beyond the city walls. A description of it by the American author Nathaniel Hawthorne[3] gives a picturesque image of the dilapidated tombs, squatters and bars along the ancient roadway:

A richly bejewelled lady

Grave monuments from Palmyra, in Syria, have a particular character all their own. Pictures of the deceased, usually carved in relief on limestone, would appear on the tomb either singly or sometimes as a pair. These images are portraits in a way, and the deceased are frequently named in an accompanying inscription in Aramaic; but they tend to have a generic look that binds them all together. Such grave markers belonged to the wealthier inhabitants whose remains would be buried in niches in a large tomb, often with scores of persons placed there together over long periods of time.

The gravestone of Tamma, daughter of Shamshigeram, portrays a beautiful young woman wearing fine cloths wound around her and numerous pieces of jewellery, including a diadem, earrings, a brooch, necklace, bracelets and rings (**fig. 143**). (Many Roman tombs had actual pieces of jewellery buried with the dead.) Tamma also holds a spindle and a distaff for spinning wool in one hand and grasps the border of her mantle with the other. Her elegant hair is swept up over her head, while long strands fall on her shoulders. Drilling was used to make the undercut areas, especially around her earrings. The rather flat treatment of hands and features and the linear approach to folds and decoration are typical of the Palmyrene style.

143 Palmyrene grave monument of Tamma, daughter of Shamshigeram. Limestone. From Palmyra. *c.* AD 100–150. H. 50 cm (1 ft 7¾ in).

144 The Via Appia with
the Tomb of Caecilia
Metella, Rome. *c.* 20 BC.

For the space of a mile or two beyond the gate of S. Sebastiano, this ancient and famous road is as desolate and disagreeable as most of the other Roman avenues. It extends over small, uncomfortable paving-stones … Here and there appears a dreary inn or a wine shop … where guests refresh themselves with sour bread and goat's milk cheese, washed down with wine of dolorous acerbity.

At frequent intervals along the roadside, up rises the ruin of an ancient tomb. As they stand now, these structures are immensely high and broken mounds of conglomerated brick, stone, pebbles, and earth, all molten by time into a mass as solid and indestructible as if each tomb were composed of a single boulder of granite. …

The tombs along the Via Appia were in fact built for prominent and wealthy Roman figures such as Caecilia Metella, one of several women of the same name in that family. One of them was married to Sulla, the general and major political force who became dictator after having defeating his enemy, Marius, in the early first century BC (see p. 22).[4] A later Caecilia Metella had a large tomb built along the Appian Way in the mid-first century BC (**fig. 144**). Its round form, ultimately derived from large-scale tumuli in Etruria, was common among substantial Roman tombs in the Republican era. The crenellations on the top are medieval but the rest of it is well-preserved Roman construction made of travertine on the exterior and rubble inside. Lord Byron, in *Childe Harold*, described it this way:

> There is a stern round tower of other days,
> Firm as a fortress, with its fence of stone,
> Such as an army's baffled strength delays,
> Standing with half its battlements alone,
> And with two thousand years of ivy grown,
> The garland of eternity, where wave
> The green leaves over all by time o'erthrown; –
> What was this tower of strength? within its cave
> What treasure lay so lock'd, so hid? – A woman's grave.
> But who was she, the lady of the dead,
> Tomb'd in a palace? Was she chaste and fair? …[5]

And the poem continues to theorize about Caecilia Metella for some time. The tomb that the emperor Augustus had built for himself was also round, as was that of Hadrian in the following century.

Burial customs varied widely, but among them was the practice of putting bronze face masks over the corpse. One depicting the face of a woman (**fig. 145**) was found on a skeleton in a tomb at Nola, not far from Naples. This seems to have been a cavalry parade mask, used during life, as indicated by the fact that the mouth is slightly open, and holes are made at the eyes where the real eyes could peer through. A thin circle of bronze outlines the pupils. Ivy decorates the sides and a scallop shell sits over each ear. Some have thought this head is that of an Amazon, a mythical female warrior, in which case it might have been worn in a parade mimicking a battle between the Greeks and the Amazons. In any case, it was used secondarily as a death mask for this particular individual. A second face mask (**fig. 146**), made of bronze covered with a thin layer of tin, has been flattened out to cover the face of the dead. The artist took great pains to show details of the rich hair, with its curls peeking out on the forehead and ringlets falling on the cheeks. Openings at the eyes, nostrils and mouth show that this one too had been used earlier as a mask for a living person.

Etruscan forebears practised cremation and also used sarcophagi for inhumation burials. Most Romans in the Republic and the early Empire were cremated and their remains put into ash urns that were either buried or placed in above-ground tombs. One practice in early times was to use a face urn, that is a clay urn with a face made on it, to hold the bones

145 Parade mask. Bronze. Found in a tomb at Nola. Second century AD. H. 25 cm (9⅞ in).

146 Face mask. Tinned bronze. Excavated in Aintab, Syria. *c.* AD 100. W. 27.5 cm (10⅞ in).

RIGHT 147 Face urn for the ashes of the dead. Clay. From Colchester, Essex. Second century AD. H. 30 cm (11¾ in).

FAR RIGHT 148 Globular urn with bones inside. Bluish-green glass. c. 50–200 AD. H. 30 cm (1 ft).

BELOW 149 Cinerary urn of Bovia Procula. Marble. First or second century AD. H. with cover 33 cm (13 in), Diam. 24 cm (9¾ in).

or ashes of the dead (**fig. 147**). Here, the face may have been thought of as connoting the whole person. Certainly the potter has gone to the trouble of incising eyebrows, beard and ears in addition to the three-dimensional eyes, nose and mouth. Frequently, bones and ashes were placed in ordinary pots or, in some cases, in glass vessels that served as funerary urns after they had previously served a useful function in the home. One such item is the bluish-green glass urn, in a globular shape with handles and a lid, that still has the bones as well as a bit of a shroud inside (**fig. 148**).

A fine example of a marble ash urn is one dedicated to Bovia Procula (**fig. 149**).[6] Delicately carved ivy leaves spring from a central vase, and birds on each side perch on the vines, pecking at the berries. The inscription says:

DIS·MANIBUS
BOVIAE·L·F
PROCVLAE
MATRI MISERRIM

To the gods of the underworld.
[Dedicated to] Bovia Procula, daughter of Lucius, a most unfortunate mother.

141

150 Cinerary urn of Vernasia Cyclas. H. 51 cm, W. 34.2 cm (20 x 13½ in).

Even through formulaic texts such as this one feels the pain of death.

Another cinerary urn takes a completely different form, one that is more architectural. The rectangular urn of Vernasia Cyclas (**fig. 150**) served as a funerary container for her ashes, and is hollow. It was set up by her husband, Vitalis, who seems to have been a freedman of the emperor, and perhaps may have been his private secretary. He is pictured with his wife on the front in the *dextrarum iunctio* position, the clasping of right hands, that was the standard way of depicting the marriage ritual (see p. 124, fig. 125). They stand within a small temporary-looking shrine that is decorated with a wreath in the pediment. This motif is repeated on the lid, where dolphins fill the corners. On a much larger scale at the figures' sides are two vertical torches from which a garland and ribbons are slung. Because this type of urn would usually stand in the niche of a tomb, the back has not been carved at all. The two sides are decorated in shallow relief with a tree, each given far less care than the scene on the front, which is probably the only part that would have been visible.

An inscription tells us that Vernasia, who was a good wife, died at a young age:

Vitalis, the freed slave and scribe working in the imperial household, [dedicates this] to his excellent wife Vernasia Cyclas, who died at the age of twenty-seven.

The three letters between the two figures, FAP, may stand for Fidelissimae (most faithful), Amantissimae (most loving) and Pientissimae (most devoted).

The torches at the corners refer to the ancient practice of carrying torches at night-time funerals, a practice that continued even when the funeral was held during the daytime. The dolphins may refer to the belief that these creatures carried the soul across the seas to joyous islands.[7] The woman holds a piece of fruit in her left hand, perhaps an apple or pomegranate. Such symbols represent life and fertility and, together with the woman's young age, suggest that she may have died due to complications from childbirth.

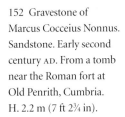

151 Tomb relief of
Lucius Antistius Sarculo
and Antistia Plutia.
Marble. H. 65 cm,
W. 95 cm (25½ x 37½ in).

152 Gravestone of
Marcus Cocceius Nonnus.
Sandstone. Early second
century AD. From a tomb
near the Roman fort at
Old Penrith, Cumbria.
H. 2.2 m (7 ft 2¾ in).

Grave markers and sarcophagi

In both the Republican and imperial periods it was customary for families of
freed slaves (freedmen) to have a communal gravestone, often embellished
with their portraits. One fine example (**fig. 151**) commemorates Lucius
Antistius Sarculo and his wife Antistia Plutia, who was a freed woman. This
commemoration was set up by two of their own freedmen, to honour them.
Their portraits are set within scallop shells surrounded by wreaths. The
man's nose had been repaired, but the repair has since been removed so that
one sees the smoothed area prepared by the restorer when he was going to
attach the new nose; the woman's new nose is still attached. The wave
(*nodus*) at the front of her hair was unfinished, or perhaps it was left rough
because it was to be painted. She wore earrings, as the holes in her ears
indicate. The elderly man has a scrawny neck and a good deal of character.
This piece has been known since at least 1510, when it was incorporated in
the wall of a house in Trastevere, Rome.[8]

Gravestones could be inscribed and decorated with scenes
honouring the dead in various ways. A large sandstone grave marker of
Marcus Cocceius Nonnus, age six, shows the boy as a victorious
charioteer holding a horse whip in one hand and a palm branch –
symbol of victory – in the other (**fig. 152**). These symbols are meant to
represent the lad as conquering death through winning a race. Found at
the edge of the Roman world, near a Roman fort in northwest England,
this is a good example of a rather roughly executed monument by a
sculptor of limited experience. Just a few lines serve to indicate the folds

153 Burial chest
of Eppia. Marble.
From Ephesus,
Turkey. H. 44 cm,
W. 84 cm, L. 79 cm
(1 ft 4 in x 2 ft 9 in
x 2 ft 7 in).

in the drapery. The letter carver incised horizontal lines into the soft stone to guide him as he wrote the rather neat inscription, whose text reads: 'To the gods of the underworld. Here lies Marcus Cocceius Nonnus, six years old.' The crude marks left in the background may originally have been covered with plaster. The family is assumed to have been granted citizenship under the emperor Marcus Cocceius Nerva (AD 96–8) and to have taken Cocceius as part of the family name, as was the custom. The son was given the emperor's name too, and therefore the piece may be dated to the early second century AD.

Under the emperor Hadrian, a change took place in burial practices, and many persons were buried in stone coffins, called sarcophagi, that were often richly decorated with mythological and decorative motifs. The word sarcophagus, meaning 'flesh-eater' in Greek, is derived from the reputed qualities of a particular reddish stone from Asia Minor that was supposed to consume the flesh of the deceased. In fact, several other materials were used for coffins, particularly marble and, less frequently, lead. Sarcophagi typically were placed in tombs along the roads outside the official limits of Roman cities; or else they were set out in the open, again, along those same roads, as seen in this view in Pompeii (**fig. 154**).

Stone sarcophagi were usually carved out roughly at the quarry and then shipped to wherever there was a market, often at places far distant. Although certain conventions tended to be repeated over and over, nonetheless each coffin has a character all its own, partly through the specific decoration and partly because of identification by an inscription or portrait. Occasionally someone is buried in a sarcophagus that has not been finished, perhaps because the family ran out of money.

154 Tombs along a road outside Pompeii.

BELOW 155 Tomb relief with the victorious Venus. Marble. AD 100–20. H. *c.* 1.22 m (4 ft).

An unusual burial chest found at Ephesus in Asia Minor (**fig. 153**) is inscribed both in Greek and Latin, as if the family of the young girl, Eppia, spoke both languages. The two inscriptions are exactly the same, and both describe her as 'not speaking': *nepia* in Greek and *infans* in Latin. Even though no precise age at death has been stated, this description indicates that she was very young. An ox head decorates the front of the sarcophagus, rams' heads ornament the corners, and garlands with many fruits and leaves hang between the heads. The sculptor's chisel marks are still visible all over the marble chest.

The imagery on sarcophagi was often meant to be uplifting, with salvation being an underlying theme. One of the recurring motifs is that of victory: victory of the soul over death, just as seen on the grave marker of Marcus Nonnus above. And to represent that idea, many coffins have carved figures of Victories – winged female figures – frequently with a garland slung between them. Or sometimes Venus can represent Victory, as on a tomb relief where the goddess is carrying a palm frond that brushes up against the right pillar (**fig. 155**). Similar to the relief with Marcus Nonnus, the palm represents victory over death. Venus's head here is a portrait of a Trajanic woman (AD 100–20), undoubtedly the deceased herself. Her portrait appears again in the centre of the arch within a scallop shell and the heads in the roundels above the capitals may represent her children. The doors at left and right, below the figure, are those of her tomb.

156 Sarcophagus of Sallustius Gelastus. Marble. Late second or early third century AD. Made in Rome. H. 38 cm, L. 1.78 m (1 ft 3 in x 5 ft 8 in).

The front of another sarcophagus, this time a child's coffin, represents a different way in which salvation may be obtained. Across the front are several cupids holding up or showing off pieces of armour (**fig. 156**).[9] The central shield, held up by a pair of cupids, gives the name of the deceased, Sallustius Gelastus, who was only five years old at the time of his death. Below the shield is a pair of cornucopiae, indicating prosperity to come in the afterlife. Cupids with weapons show in a fairly optimistic manner how the deceased is being prepared to conquer death with the aid of these pieces of armour. The collector Charles Townley bought the sarcophagus from the artist (and restorer) Giovanni Battista Piranesi in 1768.

The idea of victory may also be conveyed by a representation of a mythological story where the victory of the hero can, by implication, be transferred to victory of the deceased over death. Such oblique references to success are represented by innumerable Greek mythological stories, many of which were repeated over and over again. One such sarcophagus represented the sleeping Ariadne (**fig. 157**)[10] who was abandoned on the island of Naxos by the hero Theseus, but then was found (and wedded) by the god Bacchus. After tragic disappointment, Ariadne triumphed with an even better situation; thus (with a little imagination) she represents victory over death. Surrounding the heroine are lots of cupids flying around and making wine, thus hinting at the dionysiac connection.

BELOW 157 *Lenos* (tub sarcophagus) altered from the myth of Ariadne to the myth of Endymion. Marble. *c.* AD 250–80. Probably made in Campania. H. 62 cm, L. 2.21 m, W. 64 cm (2 ft x 7 ft 3 in x 2 ft).

158 Sarcophagus of a young girl. Carrara marble. Later second century AD. H. without lid 35.5 cm, W. 1.07 m (1 ft 2 in x 3 ft 6 in).

Interestingly, this tub-shaped sarcophagus, a *lenos*, was later altered so that the figure of the sleeping Ariadne now represented the male hero Endymion, another mythological figure who is traditionally shown sleeping. He was beloved of Luna, the moon. She so loved looking at the beautiful youth asleep that she asked her father Jupiter to give him eternal sleep, a wish that was granted. In order to change Ariadne into a man, his penis had to be attached separately but has since become detached. The sarcophagus must have been reused for a new occupant, now male; the face and hair were recarved so as to provide a portrait of the specific man.

Many sarcophagi represented neither mythological stories nor symbols of salvation, but rather created a scene from the life or death of the deceased. The coffin of a young girl (**fig. 158**)[11] poignantly represents her lying on her deathbed, surrounded by her parents (seated to right and left of the bed) and other mourners, several of them children. This scene of mourning in the home with the family surrounding the dead is called *conclamatio*.[12] In this ritual, each person called out (*conclamare*) the name of the dead, and one person closed the eyes of the deceased. The little girl's pet dog lies under the bed playing with a garland, and her slippers still rest on a stool.

The interior of the sarcophagus was carved with a headrest and two rectangular cuttings with circular depressions for the vases that would have been placed on either side of her head.[13] A third cutting was made near the other end of the coffin. The exterior ends of the sarcophagus were carved with griffins, and the back was left plain. Charles Townley bought this piece in 1768 for £20 – a sizeable sum at the time.

Egyptian painted portraits for mummies

Painted funerary portraits were common in Egypt during the Roman period, combining indigenous traditions of mummification with the Roman fascination with portraiture. Many were well preserved in a region called the Fayum, west of the Nile, that has given its name to the genre regardless of the actual findspot. The artist would paint a person's portrait in coloured wax, or sometimes tempera, on a piece of wood, and this panel would then be incorporated within the linen bindings of a mummy. Inscribed on the front of one, in Greek, are the words: 'O Artemidorus, farewell' (**fig. 159**). The mummified bones are those of a young man, as is confirmed by the portrait. Many of them can be roughly dated by their hairstyles, which tend to imitate those of the imperial family.

One example is the head of a woman (**fig. 160**) whose hairdo suggests the fashion of the empresses of the Antonine period; hence she is dated to the period of Marcus Aurelius and Lucius Verus, AD 160–80. She has exceptionally beautiful dark wide-open eyes highlighted with a spot of white and augmented by individually painted eyelashes. The lovely young lady is wearing a gilded diadem of leaves in her hair, a rich-looking necklace with emeralds and a red stone (carnelian?) set in gold, and earrings with emeralds in gold with pendent pearls. She carries her wealth with her to the grave.

A Fayum portrait of a man wearing a white tunic with purple stripes shows tremendous character (**fig. 161**). His wide face, prominent cheek bones and deep lines around the broad lips, coupled with a large nose, give him a powerful look. However, his eyes, with flesh hanging over them, look rather sad. The hairstyle suggests a date in the Trajanic period. A close look at the surface reveals several layers of colour that give a remarkably rich texture to the skin and hair. Portraits such as these give an unparalleled window into the features and personalities of Roman Egyptians, or equally Egyptian Romans.

The methods of treating death and burial in the Roman world were varied and changed considerably over time and place. But underlying them all was an effort to ease the path of the deceased on his or her journey to the afterlife, and to remember the dead with appropriate respect or affection.

9

Sources and Evidence

A study of the ancient Romans raises the question: how do we know about them. Three of the important sources, which overlapped to a certain extent, are these: ancient literature, and the information recorded by Roman authors about life in their own day; archaeological finds that help to fill in the picture of their material remains; and the collections made by travellers and others, and the studies of those objects that have made their way into museums around the world. In fact, these three sources inform each other, since ancient texts help us to understand both archaeological finds and objects in collections; and the objects illuminate the texts.

Ancient authors

Thanks to the survival of numerous texts from the Roman period, much can be gleaned about the history, daily life and culture of the Roman people. For history, one of the best sources is Livy (59 BC–AD 17), who had an agenda to support Augustus, and therefore must be regarded with caution. Nonetheless, his recording of events year by year is extremely important for piecing together the history of the Republican and early imperial periods; many books of this huge undertaking (142 books in all) have been lost, and scholars have to make do with *epitomes* or summaries. Other historians include Sallust (86–35 BC) who came from the lower classes and rose to high office before writing his history; Plutarch (*c.* AD 45–*c.* 125) who wrote biographies comparing the lives of famous Greeks and Romans; Tacitus (AD 56–*c.* 120), who wrote perhaps the most serious history of all Roman writers, concentrating on the period from the emperor Tiberius onwards; and Suetonius (late first to early second century AD), whose *Lives of the Twelve Caesars* is full of gossip and makes fascinating if sensationalist reading. Another source is called the *Scriptores Historiae Augustae*, a series of Roman authors of the fourth century AD whose biographies of second- and third-century emperors are even less reliable than those of Suetonius.

Despite the survival of some of the texts of these historians writing in Greek and Latin, much of Roman historical writing has been lost. Fortunately many other Roman writers' works have survived, and from satirists like Juvenal, lyric poets such as Catullus and comic playwrights such as Plautus, much can be learned about life among the ordinary people.

Archaeology

Excavations of Roman sites have been conducted for centuries, adding much information to our understanding of ancient peoples, whether living in towns, on farms or in country villas. Archaeology has shed light on everything from town planning to military camps to technological advances. The greatest resource for the study of the daily life of the Romans surely was the discovery in the eighteenth century of the towns of Pompeii and Herculaneum, buried under the ash and lava from the eruption of Mt Vesuvius in AD 79. The ash preserved everything from household objects to foodstuffs left on the tables as the residents fled. Houses were preserved to a certain height, and have been reconstructed in many instances to their full size. The city streets, alleys, pavements and courtyards are well preserved, and even gardens have been restored to their former appearance.

Early collecting and the Grand Tour

Before any organized collecting of large statuary began, fortuitous discoveries in fields or lakes brought attention to antiquities. Collections of small objects like coins or pots led to speculation and study. Coins speak for themselves, so collecting 'sets' of coins of emperors, particularly the twelve Caesars described by Suetonius, was (and remains) popular. Enthusiasm for antiquity spurred many of the wealthier collectors such as the Medici in Florence to acquire ancient works of art in the fifteenth century and beyond.

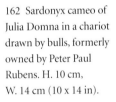

162 Sardonyx cameo of Julia Domna in a chariot drawn by bulls, formerly owned by Peter Paul Rubens. H. 10 cm, W. 14 cm (10 x 14 in).

163 Youth on Horseback. AD 1–50. Marble. Formerly in the Farnese Collection, Rome. H. 2.03 m (6 ft 8 in).

Not only nobles but also artists such as the seventeenth-century Flemish painter Peter Paul Rubens collected antiquities. He owned a sardonyx cameo thought to represent the empress Julia Domna, wife of the emperor Septimius Severus (**fig. 162**). She is shown here as the moon goddess Luna, or else *Dea Syria*, goddess of Syria, which was her native land. She rides in a chariot drawn by two bulls (compare Luna, p. 110, fig. 102). Rubens used such gems to inspire his own paintings that often treated classical subject matter and portrayed classicizing figures.

Intellectuals during the Enlightenment too were inspired by ancient Greece and Rome, and this interest sparked a fashionable new kind of travel in the eighteenth century known as the Grand Tour. This referred to trips taken by wealthy young men to Italy (usually with a companion or tutor) in order to study ancient Roman ruins and get a feel for their surroundings. (Very few women made the journey.) Although many people were interested in Greece too, especially after the publication of Stuart and Revett's *The Antiquities of Athens* in 1762, Greece at that time was considered too dangerous for travel because of the plethora of brigands that thrived there.

Like the cardinals, dukes and kings of the Renaissance, these travellers collected ancient gems and sculpture as well as objects from the natural world, and brought (or sent) them home to their town or country houses. In fact young men from the upper classes were not considered fully educated until they had completed at least one trip to Italy. Once there, they would be shown around by guides, called *ciceroni*, who might or might not be well informed.

The travellers would frequent the dealers whose shops were filled with 'antique' sculpture, often composed of ancient fragments that had been turned into full-scale statues by skilful restorers. Pieces of sculpture were often acquired in Rome from old families whose fortunes had declined so severely that they needed to sell their property to stay afloat. Many museums today are filled with the pieces brought home by the Grand Tourists who eventually either gave or sold their collections to the public institutions. The British Museum, for one, is fortunate in having had generous donors who helped to form its classical collections. The Great Court of the museum is graced, among other sculptures, by the figure of a youth on horseback wearing a military cloak (**fig. 163**). In Rome it had belonged to the Farnese – an extremely wealthy family that not only built palaces and hired major artists to decorate them, but also produced a pope (Paul III) and two cardinals. This statue was restored in the sixteenth century by the sculptor Giacomo della Porta, who replaced the many missing parts: the left front leg and both back legs, the tail, and part of the head of the horse, and much of the prince,[1] including the head, arms and right leg above the knee. The result is convincing, showing how well della Porta understood the language of classical sculpture.

Important early collectors and collections

Museums in Rome and elsewhere

Among the most important collectors in Rome were members of the Church. The popes themselves, and especially Cardinal Albani (1750–1834), ensured that many of the dealers would offer works first to them, before making them available to those on the Grand Tour. In this way the Vatican Museum as well as other collections in Rome filled rapidly with treasures from antiquity. Interestingly, pagan subject matter, including naked statues and images of ancient gods, were not off limits to these men of the cloth. The one concession to Christian modesty was that the genitals of male statues had to be covered with a fig leaf; these leaves still remain on statues in the Vatican collections today.

In Naples, the city close to Pompeii and Herculaneum, the ruler King Charles III (1716–88) considered all finds from the excavations to be his personal property. He made a royal museum at his palace in Portici at the foot of Mt Vesuvius and allowed only limited access to the finds. Many of the greatest treasures from the excavated cities are now on public view in the National Archaeological Museum of Naples because they eventually became the property of the Italian people.

The British Museum collections

The British Museum's holdings were enhanced by a colourful group of early collectors whose pieces entered the museum within the first seventy-five years of its existence. It may stand as an example of how other museums also grew in their first years, although many began at a later date. All the collectors discussed here were members of the Society of Dilettanti,[2] a learned society that did not carry the rather negative connotation that the term 'dilettante' carries today. Anyone who considered himself highly educated in the eighteenth and early nineteenth centuries would strive to be admitted to this distinguished body in London. The secretary of the society described it as follows:

> The Society of Dilettanti is something more than what Dr. Johnson defines as 'Good Fellows meeting under Certain Conditions.' It is a small private body of gentlemen, who, for 200 years, have exercised an active interest in matters connected with public taste and the arts in this country. Its members have, speaking generally, been men of education and distinction, many of whom have played a prominent part in our history.[3]

One of the major collectors whose objects came to the British Museum was Sir William Hamilton (1730–1803), British envoy to the Court of Naples from

1764 to 1800 (**fig. 164**). His collection is probably most noted for the Greek vases,[4] but he also had enormous numbers of Roman objects, many of which are illustrated in this book. Because Hamilton needed money to support his expensive lifestyle as ambassador, and also wished to have the collection in a distinguished institution, he sold it to the British Museum in 1772 for 8000 guineas, a sum that needed to be approved by an act of Parliament. These acquisitions were the first major antiquities bought by the museum and stimulated the formation of the Greek and Roman Department.

Hamilton then continued to present works to the museum, including a colossal foot, almost ninety centimetres (nearly three feet) long, wearing a sandal (**fig. 165**). Because of its size, it was undoubtedly part of a statue of a god or emperor. He

166 Bust of Hercules, of the Farnese Hercules type. Marble. Second century AD. Found at the foot of Mt Vesuvius, near Naples, and restored by Joseph Nollekens. H. 75 cm (2 ft 5½ in).

167 Portrait of Charles Townley by Christopher Hewetson. Marble. 1769. H. 56 cm (1 ft 10 in).

OPPOSITE 168 The *Discobolus*, or Discus Thrower. Marble. Roman copy of a Greek original from the fifth century BC. From Hadrian's Villa in Tivoli. H. 1.7 m (5 ft 7 in).

also gave an over life-size bust of Hercules (**fig. 166**) that was carved after the same model as the so-called Hercules Farnese, found in the Baths of Caracalla in Rome. It represented the hero, heavily bearded, and weary from having completed the last of his twelve labours. Painted on the base is a notice that it was 'found in lava at the foot of Mt. Vesuvius' and was restored by the English artist Joseph Nollekens. Hamilton himself used to climb Mt Vesuvius regularly in order to study the volcano that was repeatedly active in his day, and in fact he was the most serious vulcanologist at that time.

Another collector whose holdings made important contributions to the richness of the museum was Charles Townley (1735–1805), whose features are captured well in a portrait by the Irish sculptor Christopher Hewetson (**fig. 167**). One of his treasured acquisitions was the *Discobolus*, the 'discus thrower' (**fig. 168**). It represents a Greek athlete at the climax of his back swing with the discus, just before he changes direction and hurls it into the air. The statue was found in the emperor Hadrian's villa at Tivoli and was purchased by Townley in 1791, his last major acquisition. It appears in a painting by Johann Zoffany

169 The Townley
Collection in the Dining
Room at Park Street,
Westminster. Watercolour by
W. Chambers, 1794–5.
London. H. 39 cm,
W. 54 cm (15 x 21 in).

OPPOSITE 170 Charles
Townley's Library, an
imaginary conflation of
objects in his collection.
By Johann Zoffany. 1781–3
and 1798.

(**fig. 170**)[5] that shows the collector seated at right, accompanied by three *cognoscenti*, or knowledgeable people. Townley is surrounded by his antiquities in an imaginary configuration; the *Discobolus*, the latecomer to the collection, was added prominently in the front of the room, ten years after the rest of the picture was finished.

The *Discobolus* is one of several similar statues that are often referred to as 'Greek' because it is thought to be a Roman copy of a bronze original by a famous Greek artist, Myron, of the early fifth century BC. The ancient author Lucian (*Philopseudes* 18) identifies this type as a work of that artist. The Romans were great admirers of Greek culture in general and of their art in particular. Imitation being the highest form of flattery, they frequently copied statues for their own use in private or public spaces. Among the several Roman copies of this statue, Townley's was the first to be discovered more-or-less whole; fragments of the *Discobolus* had been discovered earlier, but had been erroneously restored as other figures.[6] The prominence of the statue was emphasized by its position at the front of the gallery, as seen in a painting of the Townley collection from the late eighteenth century (**fig. 169**).

A third major collector whose objects came to the British Museum was Richard Payne Knight (1750–1824).[7] He was fascinated by male sexuality, as seen in his remarkable book on the ancient cult of Priapus: *An Account of the Remains of the Worship of Priapus, Lately Existing at Isernia, in the Kingdom of Naples* (London: 1786).[8] The book begins with two letters, both concerning the cult of the god of sexuality and male fertility, Priapus. One is from Sir William Hamilton to Sir Joseph Banks, President of the Royal Society, and the other from a resident of the mountain village of Isernia where the cult was still thriving, in the midst of the Roman Catholic church, in the eighteenth century. The frontispiece illustrates the 'great toes' (i.e. penises) made of wax that were used as votive objects in connection with the rituals of this cult. Then, Payne Knight continues with his own disquisition 'On the Worship of Priapus'. Michaelis said of him:

> The more unreservedly we recognise Payne Knight's skill and taste in collecting, without necessarily sharing his indifference to larger marble works, the higher we are bound to estimate the result of his zeal … the greater all the while must be our [reservations] in connection with his literary activity. He made his *debut* as an author with [the book on Priapus], which deserves blame far less on account of the offensiveness of its subject than for its unsound, unmethodical, mythological fantasies. …[9]

In a chapter entitled 'Golden Age of Classic Dilettantism' Michaelis discusses the various collectors of the eighteenth century who assembled the most important collections of ancient sculpture. Segments of his poignant conclusion follow:

> [By the early nineteenth century] the excavators and the dealers, the Hamiltons and Jenkinses, had now passed away; the ranks of the collectors began to thin visibly in their turn … Sometimes there were no direct heirs to inherit the collections, sometimes the heirs did not share the interests of their predecessors, or again pecuniary circumstances might oblige the family to sell its treasures: – in any case there was but too often cause for the melancholy reflection 'how insecure is the permanency of heirlooms!' [Horace Walpole Aug. 1785]. The old race passed away, new times had dawned – who could foretell whither the tastes of the new generation might lead? It was therefore natural enough that ardent collectors, very unwilling to entertain the probability that the results of all their trouble would soon be scattered to the four winds, should seek some means of preserving their collections from such a fate … the three men who may be considered chief representatives of the Dilettanti Society at the time of its most brilliant season of activity, namely Hamilton, Townley and Knight, were yet again so far united after their death that the results of their favourite pursuits all passed into the safe keeping of the public Museum of the British nation.[10]

Three examples of collecting history

The story of how certain objects enter a museum is fascinating not only from a historical point of view, but also helps to understand the development of taste over time. By examining a few examples in the British Museum, one gets a sense of the peregrinations of single items and how they eventually make their way into public collections.

Among the great treasures of the British Museum is the glass Portland Vase (**fig. 171**), so called because it belonged for a short while to the Duchess of Portland. It has been in the British Museum since 1810, although it was formally acquired only in 1945.

According to tradition, it was originally found in 1582 in the sarcophagus of a Roman emperor, Alexander Severus.[11] It was said to be in the tomb belonging to him and his mother, Julia Mamaea, outside Rome. The vase was owned for over 150 years by the prosperous and influential Italian family, the Barberini, which is why it was formerly called the Barberini Vase. Sir William Hamilton bought it from the dealer James Byers who had acquired it from the Barberini family. But again needing money, Hamilton sold it in 1784, not long after acquiring it, to the Duchess of Portland, who died the following year. Her son bought it in the

171 The Portland Vase.
Cameo glass. *c.* AD 5–25.
Formerly in the Barberini
and Hamilton collections.
H. 24 cm, Diam. 17.7 cm
(9½ in, Diam. 7 in).

auction of her property, and loaned it to Josiah Wedgwood, the potter, who made a number of high quality copies of it. He laboured for several years to find a way to reproduce in clay what had originally been made in glass.

The subject matter of the Portland Vase is problematic and many theories have been advanced. Some think this may be a mythological story related to marriage (note the Cupid flying overhead) and the piece itself may originally have been a marriage gift. Some have seen it specifically as the marriage of Peleus and Thetis (the parents of Achilles), based partly on the fact that Thetis was a nymph associated with sea monsters, one of whom is seen by her side. According to the story, when Peleus tried to woo her, she wrestled with him, and even turned into a sea monster and several other forms, but he held on tight and finally won her over. Others think the scene was related to the birth of Octavian. Yet another theory is that it refers to Antony and Cleopatra and the battle of Actium in which those two were defeated by Octavian, who was soon to become the emperor Augustus.[12] Whichever theory one follows, it is hard to fit all the figures into the story in a logical way. One scholar has recently proposed that in fact the whole thing is a late Renaissance fabrication.[13] The multiplicity of views goes to show some of the difficulties in trying to interpret classical pieces, even those like the Portland Vase that have aroused enormous interest for centuries.

The technique used to make the cameo glass was extremely difficult and seldom used. In essence, a vessel was blown in dark blue glass, dipped in a crucible of white glass, and the two were melded together. A skilled craftsman, perhaps a gem carver, then ground down the outer level with sand or emery paste to make his figures. Some of the white areas are so thin as to allow the blue to show through. This technique is called cameo glass because it resembles the cut gemstones or tortoise shell of cameos (see figs. 13 and 162). The vase was willfully smashed in 1845 and has been reassembled with great skill several times since then.[14]

The Portland Vase, as has been noted, was brought to England by Sir William Hamilton, but the vase was never called after him. It was always either the Barberini Vase or the Portland Vase.

Another piece with a fascinating history is the Corinth Puteal, also called the Guilford Puteal. The term means a well-head, or stone for protecting a well. It was acquired by the British Museum in 1999 when it was to go up for auction at Christie's. The museum was able to forestall its sale and to collect enough money from the Heritage Lottery Fund and generous donors to acquire it for the public.[15]

It is first known in the eighteenth century to have belonged to a Turk who used it as a well-head. Its next owner was a Greek by the name of Notara, who also placed it over a well in his garden, but this time upside down to try to preserve the already damaged upper side of the marble. Notara owned a guest

172 The Corinth Puteal.
Pentelic marble. *c.* 30–10 BC.
Drawing by Simone Pomardi
for Edward Dodwell, 1805.
H. of puteal: 50 cm,
Diam. 1.06 m (19¾ in,
diam. 41¾ in).

Well of w. marble at Corinth – now in London –

house frequented by travellers, one of whom was Edward Dodwell, a distin-guished archaeologist who spent much of his life in Italy, but who also went to Greece and wrote of his travels. Dodwell described and drew the puteal and also asked his accompanying artist to draw it (**fig. 172**); thus, it was known to later generations from his records. In 1810 Frederick North (later the Earl of Guilford) bought it in Corinth and in 1813 shipped it in one of the sixty crates that he sent to his London home. Upon North's death, it was bought by Thomas Wentworth Beaumont who brought the marble to Bretton Hall, his country home in West Yorkshire, and may have deposited it in the elegant new stables of the house. Here the record stopped and by 1860, when Adolf Michaelis wrote his monumental *Ancient Marbles in Great Britain*, the whereabouts of the puteal had been lost. Eventually Bretton Hall became a teachers' training college that was later amalgamated with Leeds University. For over a century no one knew where the puteal was, or even if it still survived, but in the 1990s two art historians in Leeds wrote to the British Museum to suggest that this sculpture, being used as a planter, was ancient.

That led to its conservation and negotiated sale to a foreign buyer. But at the same time, in 2002, two more examples of the procession seen on the well-head were found in Nicopolis, the ancient town of Actium founded by Octavian after his victory over Cleopatra and Mark Antony. Suddenly the puteal could be dated and took on historical importance, meaning that the British Museum had the right to try to purchase it and keep it in Britain. This is a saga of ownership that fascinates the modern student of Roman antiquity.

The puteal is a round drum decorated in shallow relief by a procession of gods and heroes walking in two directions. In the centre where the two processions come together, Apollo with his lyre meets Minerva carrying her helmet. Both of these gods were considered protectors of Octavian. Behind Apollo come his sister Diana with her stag and perhaps Leto, their mother. Following Leto is Mercury and three dancing nymphs. In the other direction, following Minerva, walks Hercules and then a veiled woman. All are spaced out widely, and the overall style is 'neo-attic', meaning that it is a revival of the Athenian way of representing figures, mostly from the sixth century BC. This style is sometimes called 'archaizing.'

It is now clear that the monument was carved to commemorate the victory of Octavian at Actium, on the western coast of Greece. It was set up in Corinth to note this victory in another city that was favoured by Augustus because it had been re-founded by Julius Caesar, his adoptive father. The story of the Corinth Puteal is interesting both because of the use of archaizing Greek figures on a Roman monument, and because of its peregrinations, loss, and rediscovery in the late twentieth century.

Another of the celebrated objects in the museum, a recent acquisition, is the Warren Cup (**fig. 173**),[16] owned previously by Edward Perry Warren of Boston. Warren was himself a homosexual, and many of the works in his collection were erotic. While he gave many pieces to the Museum of Fine Arts, Boston, the silver cup remained with him at his country home, Lewes House, throughout his life. The cup known by his name could not be sold after his death because its subject matter was deemed too risqué by both collectors and museums. It shows two scenes of homosexual love-making between a man and a youth, one on each side. Similar subject matter is known on clay bowls that were owned by the same collector, and on a rare cameo glass vessel.[17]

In the scene of intercourse shown here, the younger man, with the aid of a strap, is lowering himself onto the older man below him. They are reclining on a mattress, but the bed itself is not shown. A lyre resting on a chest at the left alludes to the cultured setting in which the love-making is taking place. The titillating and voyeuristic effect is augmented by the young boy, a slave, who peers at one of the pairs of lovers around a partially opened door. The bearded face of the older person would have been highly unusual for a Roman of the early first century AD, when this piece was made, and suggests that the man, and the setting, are Greek.

The scenes on the cup were hammered out in the thin silver from the inside, in a technique called *repoussé*, and then further details were added by working on the outside with 'chasing'. This involves scraping to remove imperfections and to make the surface smoother, as well as incising the details with a fine tool. A plain silver liner on the inside makes it easier to clean and gives added strength to the cup. A pair of handles, now missing, would have been attached on each side. The workmanship is exceptionally fine, allowing for gentle gradations of the surfaces of the bodies and drapery.

173 The Warren Cup.
Silver. Mid-first century AD.
Said to be from Bittir
(ancient Bethther), near
Jerusalem. H. 11 cm, Diam.
9.9 cm (4¼ in, diam. 3¾ in).

Despite the refinement and quality of the silver work, the subject matter of this piece was considered inappropriate for public viewing until quite recently. Indeed it was only in the mid-1980s that a private owner dared to put it on display in the Antikenmuseum in Basel, and in the 1990s it was shown in the Metropolitan Museum in New York. Finally, with the help of public and private funds, it was bought by the British Museum in 1999 and displayed as a centrepiece of the Roman collection.

Restoration, reconstruction, and invention

Modern views of the Romans have been strongly influenced by the eighteenth century travellers and collectors of antiquities from Britain and other European countries who had been on the Grand Tour. While in Rome, such travellers would not only tour the ruins and ancient monuments, but would typically buy antiquities for their town houses or country estates back in their home country.

In order to supply this craving for antiquities, a large industry to 'create' ancient sculpture developed, and it became the practice in the restorer's studio to make a new and complete statue from what had been only a fragment dug out of the ground.

As James Dallaway described the procedure in 1800:

> The popes and cardinals of the Barbarini [sic], Borghese, and Giustiniani families, when they formed their collections from recent discoveries, exhibited only the more perfect statues, or such as were capable of restoration. The fragments and torsos were then consigned to cellars, from whence they have been extracted piecemeal by the Roman sculptors; by Cavaceppi, Cardelli, and Pacili, in particular, who have restored many of them, with wonderful intelligence and skill. The elder Piranesi was equally ingenious in composing vases and candelabra from small fragments of more exquisite workmanship.
>
> These artists have found, in several of the English nobility and gentry, a very liberal patronage. Some of those fine specimens of the arts, which are now the boast of our nation, have been obtained from them. ...[18]

The missing parts of a statue would have been carved by a modern sculptor, as indicated by Dallaway. For instance the Rondanini Faun, clashing his cymbals (**fig. 174**), has an ancient torso and right thigh from about the second century AD, but all the rest of him – his head, arms and legs – were carved in the seventeenth century by François Duquesnoy.[19] The tree stump helps to give strength to the statue because without it, the marble would not be able to support its own weight. It is a fine piece, but not much of it is ancient.

The Faun was formerly in the Rondanini Palace in central Rome, hence its name. One of the long-standing problems for those interested in keeping monuments in Italy was the acquisitive nature of British and other foreign collectors. In a fascinating passage in an early catalogue of Townley's collection, we read about the efforts of Antonio Canova, the great neoclassical sculptor, to retain this piece in Rome.

> This statue is said, some years ago, to have been sold by the Marchese Rondinini [sic] to an English nobleman, but that the influence of Canova was at that time successfully exerted to prevent its exportation from Italy. The sculptor being dead, and the Marchese become minister of police, permission for the removal of this statue was given. It was brought to England in the month of February, 1826, by Thomas Shew, Esq., of Grosvenor-place, Bath, and was purchased in the same year for the British Museum at the price of £300.[20]

Canova was more successful in preventing the Elgin Marbles of the Parthenon from being restored, an extremely important decision and an unusual view in the early nineteenth century.[21]

174 The Rondanini Faun.
An ancient torso of the
second century AD, restored
by François Duquesnoy,
1625–30. Marble. H. 1.75 m
(5 ft 9 in).

Another way of making a statue out of fragments is to put pieces together that don't belong with each other. A statue of the emperor Hadrian offering a sprig to Apollo (**fig. 175**) combines a head of Hadrian with a body to which it does not fit. The gap between the neck and the socket into which it has been placed is much too wide. This restoration was made in antiquity, showing the long history of patching parts together.

The Romans often attached pieces of sculpture to each other, sometimes because they were making a new identification of an old statue and sometimes to make whole statues from incomplete pieces. They also added pieces where the original marble block wasn't big enough or because of some changed or later intention. A good example of the latter is the head and half-length bust of a young woman wearing a wig (**fig. 176**). Some of her own hair shows underneath the wig, and its texture is clearly differentiated from the added hair. Excellent contrast is shown between the smooth face and the rougher hair, which is not polished. The wig is plaited and has slight surface cutting, but not much

175 A full-length statue of Hadrian offering a sprig of laurel to Apollo. Marble. AD 117–25. From the Sanctuary of Apollo at Cyrene. Found by Captain R. Murdoch Smith and Commander E.A. Porcher of the British Navy. H. 2.6 m (6 ft 7 in).

176 Head and bust of a young woman with a separately attached wig. Marble. AD 210–30. From the Castellani Collection. H. 71 cm (2 ft 4 in).

177 Bust of 'Clytie'.
Marble. Said to be from
near Naples. Townley
Collection. H. 57 cm
(1 ft 10½ in).

modelling, whereas the woman's own hair has
drill holes that give much more depth. The
piece was damaged from what looks like
pick marks, but she is still a beautiful and
fascinating piece of sculpture.

Some people have thought that Charles
Townley's favourite work, Clytie (**fig. 177**), is
ancient, as did he, but many consider it to be a
construct of the late eighteenth century.
A Roman statue of a Molossian hound
(**fig. 178**) was restored by the
sculptor Bartolomeo Cavaceppi,
mentioned by Dallaway, above.
Working in Rome, he ran a
highly successful studio where
numerous sculptors assisted him
in restoring ancient statuary.
Such recreated works by Cavaceppi
and others show that modern viewers
often look at ancient statues through the
eyes and craftsmanship of restorers.

178 Molossian Hound, or
'Jennings' Dog'. Marble.
Ancient sculpture restored by
Bartolomeo Cavaceppi in the
late eighteenth century.
Bought by Henry Constantine
Jennings in the 1750s.
H. 1.18 m (3 ft 10½ in).

10

The Legacy of Ancient Rome

Much has been written about the decline and fall of the Roman empire in the west, and the search for a definitive cause continues. That controversy aside, a general observer might marvel at the staying power of many of the ideas that are inherent in Roman thought.

Life in the Roman manner, albeit somewhat impoverished, seems to have continued for some time in many of the provinces in the western half of the empire, after the sack of Rome itself in AD 410. Rome's forces guarding the frontier were recalled and the northern provinces like Britannia and Germania were left open to invasion. In many cases invasion may not be the right word; occupation by small groups of 'barbarians' with considerable differences from place to place and more or less hostile attitudes toward the Romans might be a more accurate description.

A picture of the outsiders trying to join the settled life of the romanized provinces can be set against another view: that of proud tribes resisting the blandishments of Roman civilization. This division goes back to the attitudes of the local tribes at the outset of the Roman conquests, where the local elite are supposed to have preserved their status by adopting Roman values. It is claimed by some that they must have coerced their 'vassals' into acquiescing, and that a considerable tension always existed from the time of conquest (i.e. Claudius in Britain) to that of the emperor Honorius in the early fifth century, when the legions were finally withdrawn for the defence of Italy and Rome itself.[1] Much of the sophistication of Roman material culture was lost as the cohesion and interdependence of many provinces disappeared. Olives and fish sauce might no longer have been part of the diet on Hadrian's Wall, but the traders who had been looking after the needs of the camps could manage without them. They could eat local products and survive well so long as some sort of order was maintained in the district. The most lasting physical remains were constructions like the wall itself in Britain and other substantial buildings like the baths at

Trier in Germany or grand aqueducts and bridges in France and Spain, many of which, with a few repairs here and there, continued in use for centuries. The Pont du Gard near Nîmes (p. 60, fig. 52) not only continued as an aqueduct, but a roadway was added to it in the Middle Ages, allowing it to serve as a bridge.

Other less tangible aspects of Roman life carried on as well. Although the quality of life seems to have declined, an attempt to keep roads open, water flowing, and bridges repaired continued. The Christian church had been active in suppressing the cruelties of the arena and weaning the country folk, in particular, away from their pagan beliefs and observances. In this it was not wholly successful in that several saints and rituals at festivals in Greece, Italy, and Spain have a close resemblance to pre-Christian practices. For instance, the Greek rituals associated with *panegyri* celebrate saints and the Virgin with dancing and feasts that are reminiscent of ancient religious practices. Federico Fellini showed how pagan rites are still practised in Italy in his 1957 film, *The Nights of Cabiria*.

The departure of the senior legionary officers may have lead to further coarsening of the Latin language through the use of slang and dialect, thus accelerating Latin's transformation into the beginning of the Romance languages that we know today. Not that all of Cicero's or Livy's vocabulary perished; the base remained, but grammar and usage were altered. In a sense the spoken Latin language lasted in the obvious common roots that many European languages still share, despite superficial transformations. Such written texts that survived, however, were not altered at all except for copyists' errors or attempts at explanation on the page.

As far as the Church was concerned, the history of the Romans might itself be a lesson with any number of conclusions to be drawn from particular historic events. If some of the history was already invented or embroidered for the sake of a moral lesson to the Romans themselves, so much the better. Qualities like honour, duty, and faithfulness are all to be found as personal stories in the Roman author Livy's description of the founding and early days of the Roman Republic, and such qualities were promoted by the church fathers. Learned and dutiful monks patiently copied classical texts, many of which promoted the same kinds of upright values that Christianity cared for too.

Another quality that was admired by Romans and their successors alike was expressed by the term *gravitas* (literally 'weightiness'). That was the essence of restrained behaviour or speech proper to the older men, especially that of certain senators, like the older Brutus or Julius Caesar, who had gained a reputation for responsibility. Whether the historic tales are literally true or not, Livy emphasized them because he too wanted to educate and restore a moral sense to people of his own day who seemed to have lost touch with the principles that had enabled a fledgling state to succeed.

Political influence and tradition

The memory of the Romans was maintained in the political sphere by a succession of Holy Roman Emperors centred mostly in what is now Germany, although at times including many smaller European countries as well. In fact the Holy Roman Empire was a loose conglomeration of dukedoms, principalities and other forms of government, but at least figuratively each successive emperor claimed to descend from the Romans via the towering figure of the Frankish king Charlemagne, crowned on Christmas Day, AD 800. The first to bear the title of Holy Roman Emperor was Otto I (ruled AD 962–73). The idea was that he, and his successors, were claiming an inheritance from the grandeur and political power of the ancient Romans, even if the form of government and its offices had radically changed.

Roman names for magistrates were frequently taken over for some of the secular governments of medieval states, like the 'consuls' at Florence. In many places, even today, a council of senior legislators is known as the Senate. The title and office of *Procurator* has lived on in various forms in the Church and in the Law, although the duties have changed significantly from managing an imperial province. Besides the survival of specific offices that would make a rather long list, the political idea of balance that was expressed by having pairs of magistrates, either of whom could veto the other's official acts, is maintained in its most obvious form in the constitution of the United States. Here, specific parts of government are allotted different functions that allow each branch to control parts of the other two. The first French constitution brought in during the Revolution was quite specifically indebted to the form and language of the early Roman Republic; the new institution was known as the Consulate (but with only one consul) and the laws were enacted through a *senatus consulte* – exactly the language of Roman edicts. If the revolutionaries had stuck to the Roman spirit of balance, the Reign of Terror might have been avoided and the bloody rampages of the Jacobins minimized.

In the intellectual sphere, many of the classical authors were seen as educational examples in the monastic houses so that monks were officially sanctioned to copy their works in new manuscripts. The survival of a text seems to have rested on its value for the education of children being prepared for the church, government, or the military. Even pagan writers might convey desirable moral ideas or practical lessons for young scholars. This level of tolerance, even enthusiasm, ensured the preservation of a great deal of classical literature in both Greek and Latin. The Romans played their part in passing on the Greek texts as well as their own, because of their admiration for the earlier writers. Many writers of the Roman era, especially those from the hellenized provinces, wrote in Greek, and bilingual inscriptions, like that of Augustus detailing his accomplishments, are sometimes found. About the time of Hadrian, a new spirit arose in the empire that recognized its size and the heterogeneity of its inhabitants. That lead to some devaluing of Italy as the automatic centre of culture and taste, although Rome remained (for now) the seat of imperial government. A demonstration of this may lie in Hadrian's extensive travels around the empire and his issuance of a series of coins where individual provinces are celebrated by personified representations and an identifying inscription.

Curiosity about the past was one of the principal stimuli for the Renaissance, that burgeoning of scholarship, art, and science that flowered in the fifteenth and sixteenth centuries. Others included a desire to emulate the political forms of government, and the thoughts of Roman philosophers, literary figures, dramatists, and scientists, among others. Scholars promoted the detailed examination and study of the texts that had been copied so faithfully. Greek and Latin literature took prime place in this re-examination of antiquity, followed closely by philosophy and history; actual objects, especially coins and gems, were avidly collected. The interest kindled a flame for more texts, and copying of manuscripts was much increased. In architecture and the arts, too, Roman accomplishments served as models for Renaissance builders and for any number of practitioners of the fine arts, from ceramics to painting to sculpture. Donatello, Mantegna, and Michelangelo were among the greatest borrowers from antiquity but there were many others. Perhaps the biggest boost for classical scholarship came with the invention of printing in Germany and its speedy transfer to Italy, where scholars and publishers put out great numbers of 'first editions' in Venice. The preeminent publishers there were the printer Aldus Manutius and his sons. One of the revolutionary results of printing was that classical scholarship was no longer limited to the relatively few monks who transcribed ancient texts, but educated men could have their own copies of the works of ancient literary figures.

Roman history offered many examples and lessons in politics and government. Law codes in the public and private arena offered opportunities to develop civil law beside canon law and to open up a society that had been tightly controlled by the Church. Some of these changes came about more easily at some distance from the centre of control in the Vatican, just for logistical reasons, although many of the most ardent collectors and scholars were themselves luminaries of the Church, whether popes, cardinals, or bishops.

Roman law, as described in several collections of edicts and opinions, like those of Ulpian in the time of Trajan and the 'Institutes' ordered by Justinian, was examined and adopted in many jurisdictions by specific decree. A prime example from the early nineteenth century was the 'Code Napoléon', which was based heavily on Roman precedents and has been adopted in its main outlines by many jurisdictions around the world. An important exception to the general appropriation of Roman law through 'the Code' has been in England and Wales,

173

where the influence of the Anglo-Saxon tradition has been strong enough to require the development of a common law derived from the principle of judgment by a jury of equals. This is in contrast to the absolutist declaration of principles in Roman law, even though some of those are rendered fair-minded and flexible in practice by a doctrine known as *aequitas* (literally 'equity'), or fairness. This made provision for exceptions to some statutes on the grounds of likely hardship if a judgment were to be carried out to the letter of the law.

The Renaissance and beyond

If the Romans looked upon themselves with pride and nostalgia, those who came afterwards, to our own day, have admired them for many things, including their laws, government, and literature. In medieval times, Rome itself became something of a backwater and, as attacks from outsiders threatened the very survival of the city, it shrank so as to stay within the great walls built by the emperor Aurelian in the late third century AD (p. 19, fig. 8). But nevertheless, the inhabitants continued to admire the Rome of their ancestors, and eventually, in the Renaissance, Rome again became the ideal that humanists, scientists, theologians, and artists, among others, tried to emulate. Indeed, ancient Rome was in many ways the stimulus for the Renaissance, especially in Pisa and Florence, where Roman sarcophagi and sculpture served as models to early Renaissance sculptors and painters. Suddenly, with a burst of enthusiasm for understanding the physical world and reading the literature of the ancients (which had been kept alive by the monks of the Middle Ages), the intellectuals and creative artists of the day turned to the Romans as their models.

Roman traditions were never completely lost, and fascination with their accomplishments continued, and continues still, with ups and downs along the way. Politicians promoted the connections, none more than Napoleon, one of whose portraits by Ingres (**fig. 179**) shows him as a Roman emperor crowned with golden leaves. His throne rests on a rug decorated with the imperial eagle. In our own day, post-modern architecture relies heavily on classical models in piecemeal appropriations, even as it revolts against the overall systems at the same time.

Studying ancient Rome provides an unparalleled opportunity to understand the basis of modern civilization in the West. Nearly everything that came after the fall of Rome has been affected in some way by its history and traditions, whether positively or negatively, and the political and cultural milieu of the twenty-first century, two millennia after the height of the Roman empire, is still richly dependent upon it. Studying the Roman world is rewarding in countless ways, and helps those curious about the roots of culture, language, or image to achieve their goals.

179 Portrait of
Napoleon on the
imperial throne,
by Jean Auguste
Dominique Ingres
(1780–1867). Oil
on canvas. 1806.
H. 1.02 m,
W. 61 cm
(40 x 24 in).

Notes

Introduction

1 P.P. Bober and R.O. Rubinstein, with Susan Woodford, *Renaissance Artists and Antique Sculpture*, Oxford: Oxford University Press, 1986, p. 218.

2 See his *Observations on the Letter of Monsieur Mariette* (1764), published and with an introduction by John Wilton-Ely, Los Angeles: the Getty Research Institute 2002.

3 See Stephen L. Dyson, *Eugénie Sellers Strong: Portrait of an Archaeologist*, London: Duckworth 2004. See also Mary Beard, *The Invention of Jane Harrison*, Cambridge, MA: Harvard University Press 2000.

4 *Baedeker's Italy From the Alps to Naples,* 3rd edn, Leipzig: Karl Baedeker 1928, p. 250.

1 City and Citizenship

1 Paul Zanker, *The Power of Images in the Age of Augustus*, Ann Arbor: University of Michigan 1988.

2 This piece comes from the Blacas Collection, which had been formed by a father and son. The British Museum bought the whole collection in 1866. A. Michaelis, *Ancient Marbles in Great Britain*, Trans. C.A.M. Fennell, Cambridge: Cambridge University Press 1882, p. 174.

3 Dio Cassius 56.30.1–2; Tacitus, *Ann.* 1.5.

4 Suetonius, *Lives of the Twelve Caesars: Claudius* 10.2. Loeb Classical Library, 1914.

5 Ibid. *Claudius* 30.

6 Ibid. *Nero* 23.2.

7 Vol. I, Part III, pl. X.

2 The Army at Home and Abroad

1 H.H. Scullard, *From the Gracchi to Nero*, London 1963, pp. 46–76.

2 Ibid., pp. 128–9.

3 Ibid., p. 267.

4 The Tungrians were a tribe from north Holland, a subset of the *Batavi.*

5 Alan K. Bowman, *Life and Letters on the Roman Frontier: Vindolanda and its People*, London: British Museum Press 1994, pp.101–2.

6 This was the work of Giuseppe Valadier in *c.* 1830. S.B. Platner and T. Ashby, *A Topographical Dictionary of Ancient Rome*, London: Oxford University Press 1929.

7 R.P.J. Jackson and P.T. Craddock, 'The Ribchester Hoard' in B. Raftery, V. Megaw, and V. Rigby (eds.), *Sites and Sights of the Iron Age*, Oxford: Oxford University Press, 1995, pp. 78–81, fig. 48; and B.J.N. Edwards, *The Ribchester Hoard*, Preston: Lancashire County Books 1992. See also *Making History: Antiquaries in Britain 1707–2007*, eds. David Gaimster, Sarah McCarthy, Bernard Nurse, London: Royal Academy of Arts 2007, pp. 114–15.

8 British Museum translation.

9 Bowman, *Life and Letters*, p. 73.

10 Ibid. p. 134.

11 Ibid. pp. 71–2.

12 Ibid. p. 148.

13 Ibid. p. 66.

14 British Museum, P&EE 1813.12-11.1, 2.

15 A Roman mile was 1620 yards.

16 R. Embleton and Frank Graham, *Hadrian's Wall in the Days of the Romans*, New York 1984 pp. 14–15.

3 Industry, Agriculture and Communications

1 Donald Hill, *A History of Engineering in Classical and Medieval Times*, Open Court Publishing Co., La Salle, IL 1984, p. 80.

2 Trans. C.E. Van Sickle, 'The Repair of Roads in Spain under the Roman Empire', *Classical Philology* 24, January 1929, p. 78. Inscription in *CIL* II, 4697.

3 Juvenal, *Satires* 3. 236–59. Trans. Peter Green, *Juvenal The Sixteen Satires*, Harmondsworth, Middlesex: Penguin 1974.

4 A lead pipe in the British Museum (GR1856.12–26.1110) is a typical example.

5 Hill, op. cit. pp. 19–20.

6 Frontinus, *The Water Supply of the City of Rome,* Trans. Clemens Herschel, Boston 1899, p. 19.

7 Esther Boise Van Deman, *The Building of the Roman Aqueducts*, Washington: Carnegie Institution of Washington 1934, p. 4.

8 Ibid., p. 10, after Pliny, *Natural History*, 36.15 [24] 9.

9 Ibid., p. 11, and Frontinus 2.125.

10 R. Meiggs, *Roman Ostia*, Oxford: Oxford University Press 1960, pp. 54–8.

11 P. Craddock, *Early Metal Mining and Production*, Edinburgh University Press, Edinburgh 1995, p. 79; S.G. Checkland, *The Mines of Tharsis*, London: George Allen and Unwin 1967, p. 46.

12 Although the Assyrians may have had it as early as the seventh century BC. John Peter Oleson, *Greek and Roman Mechanical Water-Lifting Devices: The History of a Technology*, Toronto 1984.

13 Description based largely on Vitruvius, *The Ten Books on Architecture*, 10.7. See also *A Guide to the Exhibition Illustrating Greek and Roman Life*, London: British Museum 1908, pp. 110–11.

4 Coinage and Commerce

1 The twelve-ounce pound is still preserved today in the reckoning of the weight of gold: an ounce of gold is called a 'troy ounce', and there are twelve ounces to the pound, not sixteen.

2 Roger Bland and Catherine Johns, *The Hoxne Treasure: An Illustrated Introduction*, London: British Museum Press 1993.

3 Juvenal, *Satire* 12. 75–82. Trans. Peter Green. *Juvenal The Sixteen Satires*. Harmondsworth, Middlesex: Penguin 1974, p. 243.

4 Juvenal, *Satire 3*.

5 *A Guide to the Exhibition* 1908, p. 208.

6 J. Innes Miller, *The Spice Trade of the Roman Empire*, Oxford: Clarendon Press 1969; and A. Dalby, *Dangerous Tastes: The Story of Spices*, London: British Museum Press 2000.

7 Bowman, *Life and Letters* p. 110.

5 Spectacle and Entertainment

1 Juvenal, *Satire* 10.77–81. Trans. J. Carcopino, in *Daily Life in Ancient Rome*, New Haven: Yale University Press 1940, p. 202.

2 Loc. cit.

3 *A Guide to the Exhibition* 1908, p. 74.

4 Mark Twain, *The Innocents Abroad*, London and Glasgow: Collins 1954, p. 168.

5 Kate Ravilious, 'Gladiators Played by the Rules, Skulls Suggest', *National Geographic News*, 3 March, 2006.

6 Cicero, *Ad Familiares* 8. 4.5.

7 Tacitus, *Annales* 15.32; Suetonius, *Domitian* 4; Dio Cassius 85. 16.

8 Statius, *Thebaid* 6.455.

9 Sophocles, *Electra* lines 723–63.

10 In small letters above the horses' heads appears the name of the maker or owner of the pottery of the plaque: Anniae Arescusa.

11 Petronius, *The Satyricon*, trans. William Arrowsmith, New York: Mentor Books 1960, p. 39.

12 Augustus Hare, *Walks in Rome*, London: 1909, p. 265.

13 William Smith, *A Dictionary of Greek and Roman Antiquities*, London: 1854, p. 145. The source was Lampridius, an author in the *Historiae Augustae*.

14 An athlete's bronze toilet set, found near Düsseldorf in Germany, includes an aryballos (oil or perfume jar) and two strigils with a ring for hanging them on the wall.

15 Garrett G. Fagan, *Bathing in Public in the Roman World*, Ann Arbor: University of Michigan Press 1999, pp. 24–9.

16 Garret G. Fagan, 'Interpreting the Evidence: Did Slaves Bathe at the Baths?' in De Laine and Johnston pp. 25–34.

6 Religions, Near and Far

1 A description of its finding by the child, Isabel Cutter and her friend Hester Skipsey, is recorded in an early court dispute over ownership of the tray. Isabel's father, the blacksmith, sold it in two pieces (the foot first) to a goldsmith in Newcastle, a Mr Isaac Cookson. The Duke of Somerset claimed the piece to be his property, as it was treasure trove that was his by right as lord of the manor of Corbridge. The blacksmith was fined 6 pence for not having revealed it to the duke. The goldsmith refused to give it up, even though he was offered in cash the £33 6s that he had paid for it; but eventually he accepted payment, and the Duke of Somerset and of Northumberland deposited it at the British Museum until it was eventually bought by them in 1993. Francis Haverfield, 'Roman Silver in Northumberland', *Journal of Roman Studies* 1914, pp. 6–8.

2 Tesserae are the small square stones or sometimes glass pieces used to make a mosaic. The word comes from the Greek word 'four', referring to the four-sided shape.

3 T.W. Potter and Catherine Johns, *Roman Britain*, London 1992, p. 173.

4 British Museum, P & EE 1978. 01-02.80. Second to fourth century AD. Translation courtesy of the British Museum.

5 Roger Tomlin, *Tabellae Sulis: Roman Inscribed Tablets of Tin and Lead from the Sacred Spring at Bath*, Oxford: Oxford University Press 1988; and R.S.O. Tomlin, 'The Curse Tablets', in *The Temple of Sulis Minerva at Bath*, Oxford: Oxford University Committee for Archaeology 1988.

6 Ibid. p. 149.

7 The sow and Lanuvium lead to the founding of Rome.

8 Previously called the Temple of Fortuna Virilis.

9 Bronze leg: GR1772.03–05.60, Hamilton Collection; marble relief of a leg: GR1867.05-08.117, Blacas Collection.

10 She appears that way on the side of the Arch of Constantine. B. Andreae, *The Art of Rome*, New York: Harry N. Abrams 1977, fig. 624.

11 MacMullen, Ramsay, *Paganism in the Roman Empire*, New Haven: Yale University Press 1981, pp. 122 ff.

12 GR1873.08–20.260; Br 904. *Ca.* AD 200.

13 R. Turcan, *The Cults of the Roman Empire*, trans. Antonia Nevill, Blackwell: Malden, MA 1996, pp. 67–8.

14 GR 1974.07–23.1 Lamp Q1384. Said to be from Mitcham, Surrey. *c.* AD 175–225.

15 R.E. Witt, *Isis in the Graeco-Roman World*, Cornell University Press, Ithaca, NY 1971, especially pp. 70–88 and 127. An inscription in the British Museum linked an Isis at Athens with Demeter. AD 126–30. GR 1816.06–10.165 (Elgin Collection); Ins. 57.

16 See the bronze sistrum, said to have been found in the River Tiber, in the case nearby: GR1893.06–26.1. The decoration here shows the story of Romulus and Remus being suckled by the wolf (see Chapter 2, the Fulham Sword, p. 45).

17 A marble disc with Serapis represents him in his role as Helios-Serapis, god of the Sun. GR 1929.04–19.1.

18 Townley manuscript; quoted in A.H. Smith, p. 4. This restorer was the son of Bartolomeo Cavaceppi. The bust of this piece is modern.

19 *Roman Inscriptions in Britain* [RIB] 658 (74).

20 Dated AD 400–500. GR 1982.03-02.9; Lamp Q 1434 ter.

21 A. Seager, in G.M.A. Hanfmann, *Sardis from Prehistoric to Roman Times*, Cambridge, MA: Harvard University Press 1983, p. 172.

22 J. S. Crawford, *The Byzantine Shops* (Archaeological Exploration of Sardis Monograph 9), Cambridge, MA: Harvard University Press 1990, p. 1.

7 The Household

1 Phallus rings: GR1872.06–04.340 and 341; 1980.03-01.1 and 2.

2 Susan Walker, *Roman Sarcophagi in the British Museum*, London: British Museum Press 1990, Monograph 4, p. 16.

3 The bronze needles: GR 1772.03–12.31 and 34; GR 1887.11–01.23. The bone pin, GR 1772.03–11.107. On the comb of Modestina, the second letter after her name has been read as H. In that case she should be regarded as H[onesta].

4 Bowman, *Life and Letters*, pp. 71 and 135.

5 The text, *non tibi Tyndaridis facies invisa Lacaenae* (2. 601), is one of the earliest surviving texts of Vergil.

6 Baby feeder: GR 1856.12–26.422.

7 Five dice in different colours and sizes: steatite, GR 1980.04–01.3; bone, GR 1865.12–14.68; marble, GR 1772.03–11.238; rock crystal, 1923.04–01.1187; and agate, GR 1814.07–04.1088.

8 GR 1772.03–11.250.

9 *Museum Britannicum*, London 1778, p. 44, note.

10 GR 1814.0.7–04.1083; GR 1859.03–01.48; and GR 1873.08–20.647, respectively.

11 GR 1873.05–05.150.

12 Petronius, *Satyricon* 35–6. Trans. William Arrowsmith. Ann Arbor: University of Michigan Press 1959, pp. 32–3.

13 Fluted bowl: GR 1890.09–23.4; silver 168. Serving dish with swastika: GR 1889.10–19.19; silver 154. Plate with Mercury: GR 1890.09–23.1; silver 150.

14 Catherine Johns, *Arretine and Samian Pottery*, London: British Museum Publications 1977, pl. 1.

15 The mould for one of them is stamped M[arcus] PEREN[nius]. GR 1896.12-17.1. The scene represents a lion hunt. Johns, op. cit. pl. 15.

16 James Higginbotham, *Piscinae: Artificial Fishponds in Roman Italy*, Chapel Hill, NC 1997, pp. 159–63.

17 GR 1814.07–04.712; GR 1856.12–26.1008; and GR 1856.12–26.669 respectively.

8 Health, Death and the Afterlife

1 John Scarborough, 'The Background of Hellenistic Medicine', *Roman Medicine*, Ithaca: Cornell University Press, pp. 26–51.

2 Garrett G. Fagan, *Bathing in Public in the Roman World*, Ann Arbor 1999, pp. 85–103.

3 Quoted by Augustus Hare in his *Walks in Rome* (1909) p. 297.

4 H.H. Scullard, *From the Gracchi to Nero*, New York: 1959, p. 83.

5 Lord Byron, *Childe Harold's Pilgrimage*, stanzas 99–100.

6 The lid is modern.

7 Taylor Combe, *Ancient Marbles* Vol. V, pp. 9–10.

8 British Museum Sculpture Catalogue p. 290.

9 Susan Walker, *Roman Sarcophagi*, Cat. 28, p. 30.

10 Ibid. Cat. 43, p. 38.

11 Ibid. Cat. 6, p. 17.

12 Jocelyn Toynbee, *Death and Burial in the Roman World*, London 1971, p. 44.

13 Walker, *Roman Sarcophagi*, p. 17 and fig. 1.

9 Sources and Evidence

1 Thought to be a Julio-Claudian prince.

2 Lionel Cust, *History of the Society of Dilettanti*, Sidney Colvin, ed., London: Macmillan 1914.

3 Cecil Harcourt-Smith, *The Society of Dilettanti: Its Regalia and Pictures*, London: Macmillan 1932, p. 1.

4 Ian Jenkins and Kim Sloan, *Vases and Volcanoes*, London: British Museum Press 1996.

5 Johann Zoffany, *Charles Townley and his Collection*, 1781. Townley Hall Art Gallery and Museums, Burnley Borough Council, Burnley.

6 Seymour Howard, 'Some Eighteenth-Century Restorations of Myron's Discobolos', *Antiquity Restored: Essays on the Afterlife of the Antique*, Vienna: IRSA 1990, pp. 70–77.

7 Michael Clarke and Nicholas Penny, eds. *The Arrogant Connoisseur: Richard Payne Knight 1751–1824*, Manchester: Manchester University Press 1984.

8 A newer edition was published by the Society of Dilettanti, *c.* 1900, 'Privately printed for members only.'

9 Michaelis, *Ancient Marbles*, pp. 119 and 121–2.

10 Ibid. pp. 126–8 (excerpted).

11 The sarcophagus is in the Capitoline Museum.

12 Susan Walker, *The Portland Vase*, London 2004, p. 41; Jenkins and Sloan, *Vases and Volcanoes*, pp. 187–91. W. Gudenrath, K. Painter, and D. Whitehouse, 'The Portland Vase', *Journal of Glass Studies* 32 (1990) pp. 14–188. Robin Brooks, *The Portland Vase: The Extraordinary Odyssey of a Mysterious Roman Treasure*, New York: Harper Collins 2004. D.E.L. Haynes, *The Portland Vase* (rev. 2nd edn, London 1975). On the theories of meaning: Susan Woodford, *Images of Myths in Classical Antiquity*, Cambridge: Cambridge University Press 2003.

13 Jerome Eisenberg, *Minerva* 14 (2003) pp. 37–41.

14 Nigel Williams, *The Breaking and Remaking of the Portland Vase*, London: British Museum Press 1989.

15 http://www.artfund.org/artwork/8907/corinths-monument-to-actium-the-guildford

16 Dyfri Williams, *The Warren Cup*, London: British Museum Press 2006; John R. Clarke, *Looking at Lovemaking*, Berkeley 1998, pp. 61–78.

17 Ibid. pp. 76–77 and 79–82.

18 Dallaway, *Anecdotes of the Arts*, p. 272.

19 François Duquesnoy (1597–1643), called Il Fiamingo [the Flemish man] by the Italians, restored the statue between 1625 and 1630. He '…wanted to show himself a rigorous imitator of the Greek manner…', according to one of his biographers, Giovanni Battista Passeri. See Estelle Lingo, 'The Greek Manner and a Christian *Canon*: François Duqesnoy's *Saint Susanna*,' in *The Art Bulletin* 84.1 (Mar. 2002) p. 65.

20 Ellis, *Townley Gallery* 1846 p. 239.

21 Jenkins, *Archaeologists and Aesthetes* p. 29 and p. 232 note 57.

10 The Legacy of Ancient Rome

1 Several views on this topic are expressed in D.J. Mattingly, ed. *Dialogues in Roman Imperialism, Journal of Roman Archaeology* supplement 23, 1997.

179

Bibliography

General and Introduction

A Guide to the Exhibition Illustrating Greek and Roman Life. London: British Museum 1908.

Aicher, Peter J. *Rome Alive: A Source-Guide to the Ancient City* Vols. I–II. Wauconda, IL: Bolchazy-Carducci Publishers 2004.

Burn, Lucilla. *The British Museum Book of Greek and Roman Art.* London: British Museum Press 1991.

Claridge, Amanda. *Rome.* [Oxford Archaeological Guides] Oxford: Oxford University Press 1998.

Cook, B.F. *Greek and Roman Art in the British Museum.* London: British Museum Press 1976.

Cornell, Tim and John Mathews. *Atlas of the Roman World.* New York: Checkmark Books 1982.

Coulston, Jon and Hazel Dodge, eds. *Ancient Rome: The Archaeology of the Eternal City.* Oxford: Oxford University School of Archaeology 2000.

Cyrino, Monica Silveira. *Big Screen Rome.* Malden, MA: Blackwell Publishing 2005.

Favro, Diane. *The Urban Image of Augustan Rome.* Cambridge: Cambridge University Press 1996.

Jenkins, Ian. *Greek and Roman Life.* Cambridge, MA: Harvard University Press 1986.

Joshel, Sandra R., Margaret Malamud, and Donald T. McGuire, Jr, eds. *Imperial Projections.* Baltimore: Johns Hopkins University Press 2005.

Kleiner, Fred S. *A History of Roman Art.* Belmont, CA: Thomson/Wadsworth 2007.

Potter, D.S. and D.J. Mattingly, eds. *Life, Death, and Entertainment in the Roman Empire.* Ann Arbor, MI: University of Michigan Press 1999.

Potter, Timothy W., and Catherine Johns. *Roman Britain.* London: British Museum Press 1992.

Ramage, Nancy H. and Andrew Ramage. *Roman Art: Romulus to Constantine* (5th edn). Upper Saddle River, NJ: Prentice Hall 2009.

Scarre, C. *Chronicle of the Roman Emperors: The Reign-By-Reign Record of the Rulers of Imperial Rome.* London: Thames and Hudson 1995.

Shelton, Jo-ann. *As the Romans Did.* New York: Oxford University Press 1988.

Solomon, Jon. *The Ancient World in the Cinema.* New Haven and London: Yale University Press 2001.

Stambaugh, John E. *The Ancient Roman City.* Baltimore: The Johns Hopkins University Press 1988.

Walker, Susan. *Roman Art.* London: British Museum Press 1991.

Wilson, David. *The British Museum: A History.* London: British Museum Press 2002.

1 City and Citizenship

Bauman, Richard A. *Women and Politics in Ancient Rome.* London: Routledge 1992.

Crook, J.A. *Law and Life of Rome 90 BC–AD 212.* Ithaca, NY: Cornell University Press 1967.

Duncan-Jones, Richard. *Money and Government in the Roman Empire.* Cambridge: Cambridge University Press 1994.

Levick, Barbara. *Government of the Roman Empire: A Sourcebook* (2nd edn). New York: Routledge 2000

Syme, Ronald. *The Roman Revolution.* Oxford: Oxford University Press 1939.

Zanker, Paul. *The Power of Images in the Age of Augustus.* Ann Arbor, MI: University of Michigan Press 1988.

2 The Army at Home and Abroad

Abdy, Richard. *The British Museum Pocket Dictionary of the Roman Army.* London: British Museum Press 2008.

Beard, Mary. *The Roman Triumph.* Cambridge: Cambridge University Press 2007.

Birley, Anthony. *Garrison Life at Vindolanda: A Band of Brothers.* Stroud, Gloucestershire: Tempus Publishing 2002.

Birley, Robin. *On Hadrian's Wall: Vindolanda: Roman Fort and Settlement.* London: Thames and Hudson 1977.

Bowman, Alan K. *Life and Letters on the Roman Frontier: Vindolanda and its People.* London: British Museum Press 1998.

Campbell, J.B. *The Roman Army, 31 BC–AD 337: A Sourcebook.* London: Routledge 1994.

Hanson, William and Gordon Maxwell. *Rome's North West Frontier: The Antonine Wall.* Edinburgh: Edinburgh University Press 1983.

Watson, G.R. *The Roman Soldier.* Ithaca, NY: Cornell University Press 1969.

3 Industry, Agriculture and Communications

Adam, Jean-Pierre. *Roman Building: Materials & Techniques.* Trans. Anthony Mathews. Bloomington, IN: Indiana University Press 1994.

Casson, Lionel. *Ships and Seamanship in the Ancient World.* Princeton: Princeton University Press 1971.

Chevalier, Raymond. *Roman Roads.* Trans. N.H. Field. London: B.T. Batsford Ltd 1989.

Craddock, Paul T. *Early Metal Mining and Production.* Washington: Smithsonian 1995.

Healy, John F. *Mining and Metallurgy in the Greek and Roman World.* London: Thames and Hudson 1978.

Hill, Donald. *A History of Engineering in Classical and Medieval Times.* La Salle, IL: Open Court Publishing Company 1984.

Hodge, A. Trevor. *Roman Aqueducts & Water Supply.* London: Duckworth 2002.

Koloski-Ostrow, Ann Olga, ed. *Water Use and Hydraulics in the Roman City.* Dubuque, Iowa: Kendall/Hunt Publishing Co. 2001.

O'Connor, Colin. *Roman Bridges.* Cambridge: Cambridge University Press 1993.

Oleson, John Peter. *Greek and Roman Mechanical Water-Lifting Devices: The History of a Technology.* Toronto: University of Toronto Press 1984.

Sear, Frank B. *Roman Architecture.* Ithaca, NY: Cornell University Press 1983.

Taylor, Rabun. *Roman Builders: A Study in Architectural Process.* Cambridge: Cambridge University Press 2003.

White, K.D. *Greek and Roman Technology.* Ithaca, NY: Cornell University Press 1984.

4 Coinage and Commerce

Abdy, Richard A. *Romano-British Coin Hoards.* Princes Risborough: Shire Publications 2003.

Bland, Roger and Catherine Johns. *The Hoxne Treasure: An Illustrated Introduction.* London: British Museum Press 1993.

Burnett, Andrew. *Coinage in the Roman World.* London: Seaby 1987.

Crawford, Michael H. *Roman Republican Coinage* Vols. I and II. Cambridge: Cambridge University Press 1991.

Dodge, Hazel and Bryan Ward-Perkins, eds. *Marble in Antiquity. Collected Papers of J.B. Ward-Perkins* (Archaeological Monographs of the British School at Rome 6). London: British School at Rome 1992.

Duncan-Jones, Richard. *Structure and Scale in the Roman Economy.* Cambridge: Cambridge University Press 1990

Eagleton, Catherine and Jonathan Williams, eds. *Money: A History.* London: British Museum Press 1997.

Greene, Kevin. *The Archaeology of the Roman Economy.* Berkeley and Los Angeles: The University of California Press 1990.

Hayes, John W. *Handbook of Mediterranean Roman Pottery.* London: British Museum Press 1997.

Kent, J.P.C. *Roman Coins.* New York: Harry N. Abrams, Inc. 1978.

Miller, J. Innes. *The Spice Trade of the Roman Empire 29 BC–AD 641.* Oxford: Oxford University Press 1969.

Mattingly, Harold, and E.A. Sydenham. *Roman Imperial Coinage.* London: British Museum (Numerous publication dates and reprints by Spink & Son.)

Peacock, D.P.S. *Pottery in the Roman World: An Ethnoarchaeological Approach.* London and New York: Longman 1982.

Peacock, D.P.S. and D.F. Williams. *Amphorae and the Roman Economy: An Introductory Guide.* London and New York: Longman 1986.

5 Spectacle and Entertainment

DeLaine, J. and D.E. Johnson, eds. *Roman Baths and Bathing: Proceedings of the First International Conference on Roman Baths* Part 1: Bathing and Society. *Journal of Roman Archaeology* supplementary series 37.

Fagan, Garrett G. *Bathing in Public in the Roman World.* Ann Arbor: University of Michigan Press 1999.

Humphrey, John H. *Roman Circuses: Arenas for Chariot Racing.* Berkeley: University of California Press 1986.

Kohne, E. and C. Ewigleben, eds. *Gladiators and Caesars: The Power of Spectacle in Ancient Rome.* London: British Museum Press 2000.

Welch, Katherine E. *The Roman Amphitheatre: From Its Origins to the Colosseum.* Cambridge: Cambridge University Press 2006.

Winkler, Martin M. *Gladiator: Film and History.* Malden, MA: Blackwell Publishing 2005.

Yegül, Fikret K. *Baths and Bathing in Classical Antiquity.* Cambridge: MIT Press 1992.

6 Religions, Near and Far

Armour, Robert A. *Gods and Myths of Ancient Egypt* (2nd edn). Cairo and New York: American University in Cairo Press 2001.

Gager, John G., ed. *Curse Tablets and Binding Spells from the Ancient World.* Oxford: Oxford University Press 1992.

MacDonald, William L. *The Pantheon.* Cambridge: Harvard University Press 1976.

MacMullen, Ramsay. *Paganism in the Roman Empire.* New Haven and London: Yale University Press 1981.

Rives, James B. *Religion in the Roman Empire.* Malden, MA: Blackwell Publishing 2007.

Small, Alastair, ed. *Subject and Ruler: The Cult of the Ruling Power in Classical Antiquity. Journal of Roman Archaeology,* supplement 17. Ann Arbor 1996.

Turcan, Robert. *The Cults of the Roman Empire.* Trans. Antonia Nevill. Oxford: Blackwell 1996.

Turcan, Robert. *The Gods of Ancient Rome: Religion in Everyday Life from Archaic to Imperial Times.* Edinburgh: Edinburgh University Press 2000.

Ulansey, David. *The Origins of the Mithraic Mysteries: Cosmology and Salvation in the Ancient World.* Oxford: Oxford University Press 1991.

Walker, Susan, ed. *Ancient Faces: Mummy Portraits from Roman Egypt.* New York: The Metropolitan Museum of Art and Routledge 2000.

Witt, R.E. *Isis in the Graeco-Roman World.* Ithaca, NY: Cornell University Press 1971.

7 The Household

Carcopino, Jerome. *Daily Life in Ancient Rome* (2nd edn). New Haven: Yale University Press 2003.

Ciarallo, Annamaria and Ernesto De Carolis, eds. *Pompeii: Life in a Roman Town.* Milan: Electa 1999.

Clarke, John R. *The Houses of Roman Italy, 100 BC–AD 250: Ritual, Space, and Decoration.* Berkeley: University of California Press 1991.

Clarke, John R. *The Lives of Ordinary Romans: Visual Representation and Non-Elite Viewers in Italy, 100 BC–AD 315.* Berkeley: University of California Press 2003.

D'Ambra, Eve. *Roman Women.* Cambridge: Cambridge University Press 2007.

Dunbabin, K.M.D. *The Roman Banquet: Images of Conviviality*. Cambridge: Cambridge University Press 2003.

Fantham, Elaine, and Helene Peet Foley, Natalie Boymel Kampen, Sarah B. Pomeroy, and H. Alan Shapiro. *Women in the Classical World*. New York and Oxford: Oxford University Press 1994.

Gazda, Elaine, ed. *Roman Art in the Private Sphere: New Perspectives on the Architecture and Decor of the Domus, Villa, and Insula*. Ann Arbor, MI: University of Michigan Press 1991.

Johns, Catherine. *Arretine and Samian Pottery*. London: British Museum Press 1977.

Lefkowitz, Mary R. and Maureen B. Fant. *Women's Life in Greece and Rome*. Baltimore: Johns Hopkins University Press 2005.

MacKendrick, Paul. *The Mute Stones Speak*. London and New York: Methuen 1960.

Saller, Richard P. *Patriarchy, Property and Death in the Roman Family*. Cambridge: Cambridge University Press 1996.

Wallace-Hadrill, Andrew. *Houses and Society in Pompeii and Herculaneum*. Princeton: Princeton University Press 1994.

8 Health, Death and the Afterlife

Cruse, Audrey. *Roman Medicine*. Stroud: Tempus 2004.

Huskinson, Janet. *Roman Children's Sarcophagi: Their Decoration and Social Significance*. Oxford: Oxford University Press 1996.

Jackson, R. 'Roman Doctors and their Instruments: Recent Research Into Ancient Practice.' *Journal of Roman Archaeology* 3 (1990) pp. 5–27.

King, Helen. *Greek and Roman Medicine*. London: Bristol Classical Press 2001.

McCann, Anna Marguerite. *Roman Sarcophagi in the Metropolitan Museum of Art*. New York: Metropolitan Museum of Art 1978.

Scarborough, John. *Roman Medicine*. Ithaca: Cornell University Press 1969.

Toynbee, Jocelyn. *Death and Burial in the Roman World*. London: Thames and Hudson 1971.

Walker, Susan. *Roman Sarcophagi in the British Museum*. London: British Museum Press 1990.

9 Sources and Evidence

Bober, Phyllis Pray, and Ruth O. Rubinstein, with contributions from Susan Woodford. *Renaissance Artists and Antique Sculpture: A Handbook of Sources*. Oxford: Oxford University Press 1986.

Chambers, Neil. *Joseph Banks and the British Museum: The World of Collecting, 1770–1830*. London: Pickering & Chatto 2007.

Clarke, John R. *Looking at Lovemaking: Constructions of Sexuality in Roman Art 100 B.C.–AD 250*. Berkeley: University of California Press 1998.

Clarke, Michael, and Nicholas Penny, eds. *The Arrogant Connoisseur: Richard Payne Knight 1751–1824*. Manchester: Manchester University Press 1984.

Coltman, Viccy. *Fabricating the Antique: Neoclassicism in Britain, 1760–1800*. Chicago: University of Chicago Press 2006.

Cook, B.F. *The Townley Marbles*. London: British Museum Press 1985.

Dallaway, James. *Anecdotes of the Arts in England: or, Comparative Remarks on the Architecture, Sculpture, and Painting*. London: T. Cadell and W. Davies 1800.

de Beer, G.R. *Sir Hans Sloane and the British Museum*. London: British Museum Press 1953.

Dyson, Stephen L. *In Pursuit of Ancient Pasts: A History of Classical Archaeology in the Nineteenth and Twentieth Centuries*. New Haven: Yale University Press 2006.

Edwards, E. *Lives of the Founders of the British Museum*. London: Trübner 1870.

Ellis, Sir Henry. *The Townley Gallery of Classic Sculpture in the British Museum* Vols. I–II. London: M.A. Nattali 1846.

Fothergill, Brian. *Sir William Hamilton Envoy Extraordinary*. London: Faber and Faber 1969.

Greenhalgh, Michael. *The Survival of Roman Antiquities in the Middle Ages*. London: Duckworth and Company, Ltd. 1989.

Grossman, Janet B., Jerry Podany, and Marion True, eds. *History of Restoration of Ancient Stone Sculptures*. Los Angeles: J. Paul Getty Museum 2003.

Haskell, Francis and Nicholas Penny. *Taste and the Antique*. New Haven: Yale University Press 1981.

Hermann, Frank. *The English as Collectors: A Documentary Sourcebook*. New Castle, Delaware: Oak Knoll Press, and London: John Murray 1999.

Jenkins, Ian. *Archaeologists and Aesthetes in the Sculpture Galleries of the British Museum 1800–1939*. London: British Museum Press 1992.

Jenkins, Ian, and Kim Sloan. *Vases and Volcanoes: Sir William Hamilton and his Collection*. London: British Museum Press 1996.

Jenkyns, Richard. *The Legacy of Rome: A New Appraisal*. Oxford: Oxford University Press 1992.

Michaelis, Adolf. *Ancient Marbles in Great Britain*. Trans. C.A.M. Fennell. Cambridge: Cambridge University Press 1882.

Scott, Jonathan. *The Pleasures of Antiquity: British Collectors of Greece and Rome*. New Haven: Yale University Press 2003.

Sloan, Kim. *Enlightenment: Discovering the World in the Eighteenth Century*. London: British Museum Press 2003.

Williams, Dyfri. *The Warren Cup*. London: British Museum Press 2006.

10 The Legacy of Ancient Rome

Ridley, Ronald T. *The Eagle and the Spade: The Archaeology of Rome During the Napoleonic Era, 1809–1814*. Cambridge: Cambridge University Press 1991.

British Museum Catalogues

Bailey, D.M. *Catalogue of the Lamps in the British Museum* Vols. II–IV. London: British Museum 1975–96.

Burn, Lucilla, and Reynold Higgins. *Catalogue of Greek Terracottas in the British Museum*, Vol. III. London: British Museum Press 2001.

Combe, Taylor, *et al. A Description of the Collections of Ancient Marbles in the British Museum*. 11 vols. London: British Museum 1812–61.

Grueber, H.A. *Coins of the Roman Republic in the British Museum*. London: British Museum 1910.

Hinks, R.P. *Catalogue of the Greek Etruscan and Roman Paintings and Mosaics in the British Museum*. London: British Museum 1933.

Mattingly, Harold. *Coins of the Roman Empire in the British Museum*. London: British Museum 1923–65.

Smith, A.H. *Catalogue of Sculpture in the Department of Greek and Roman Antiquities*. Vols I–III. London: British Museum 1892–1901.

Walters, H.B. *Catalogue of the Bronzes Greek, Roman and Etruscan in the Department of Greek and Roman Antiquities, British Museum*. London: British Museum 1899.

Walters, H.B. *Catalogue of the Engraved Gems and Cameos Greek, Etruscan and Roman in the British Museum*. London: British Museum 1926.

Walters, H.B. *Catalogue of the Greek and Roman Lamps in the British Museum*. London: British Museum 1914.

Walters, H.B. *Catalogue of the Terracottas in the Department of Greek and Roman Antiquities, British Museum*. London: British Museum 1903.

Photography © The Trustees of the British Museum unless otherwise noted.

p. 1 GR 1805,0703.153 (Sculpture 2317), CM 1994,0401.1–400; **p. 2** GR 1989,0322.1; **p. 5** GR 1867,0510.4 (Bronze 1611); **p. 7** BM (photos P.J. Williams/S. Peckham, Dudley Hubbard); **Fig. 1** Museo Capitolino, Rome (© Photo Scala, Florence); **2** Technical Art Services (TAS); **3** TAS; **4** GR 1968,0627.1; **5** CM 3864; **6** Collection of the authors; **7** TAS; **8** TAS; **9** BM (photo P.J. Williams/S. Peckham); **10** BM (photo P.J. Williams/S. Peckham); **11** CM I.542.4136; **12** GR 1911,0901.1; **13** GR 1867,0507.484 (Gem 3577); **14** GR 1856,1226.1722 (Sculpture 1990); **15** PE 1965,1201.1; **16** GR 1850,0304.35 (Sculpture 1890); **17** GR 1874,0712.11 (Sculpture 1893); **18** PE 1848,1103.1; **19** GR 1861,1127.19 (Sculpture 1463); **20** GR 1861,1127.15 (Sculpture 1464); **21** GR 1861,1127.15 (Sculpture 1911); **22** GR 1805,0703.102 (Sculpture 1917); **23** CM 1867,0101.865; **24** GR 1839,0214.9; **25** GR 1887,0725.31 (Sculpture 2001); **26** GR 1962,0824.1; **27** PE 1866,1229.21–4; **28** GR 1856,1226.1621 (Painting 37); **29** GR 1867,0508.644; **30** GR 1772,0302.152 (Bronze 1524); **31** GR 1805,0703.317 (Terracotta D 633); **32** GR 1930,0419.1; **33** BM (photo P.J. Williams/S. Peckham); **34** GR 1804,0703.307 (Terracotta D 569); **35** GR 1805,0703.342 (Terracotta D 625); **36** GR 1973,0330.5 (Sculpture 1772); **37** GR 1867,0510.4 (Bronze 1611); **38** PE 1814,0705.1; **39** Society of Antiquaries, London; **40** PE 1883,0407.1; **41** EA 5473; **42** GR 1973,0422.1 (Sculpture 2271); **43** PE 1986,1001.64; **44** PE 1813,1211.1–2; **45** Photo © Robert Harding World Imagery; **46** Photo © Roy and Lesley Adkins; **47** PE 1883,0725.1; **48** *Antichità Romane*, 1756, vol. III, pl. 7, p. 284 (photo © British Library); **49** Photo Michael H. Ramage; **50** Photo N.H. Ramage; **51** Photo © iStockphoto. com/Jivko Kazalov; **52** Photo © Robert Harding World Imagery; **53** TAS; **54** Photo N.H. Ramage; **55** BM (photo P.J. Williams/S. Peckham); **56** GR 1889,0622.1; **57** TAS; **58** GR 1892,0517.1 (Bronze 2573); **59** CM BMC 2; **60** CM 1867,0212.1; **61** CM RRC 25; **62** CM 1994,0401.1–400; **63** CM 1756,0101.1132; **64** CM BMC 132; **65** BM (photo P.J. Williams/S. Peckham); **66** GR 1975,1107.1; **67** GR 1805,0703.458 (Sculpture 2213); **68** GR 1850,0304.32 (Sculpture 2212); **69** GR 1805,0703.457 (Sculpture 2212); **70** GR 1772,0319.1 (Bronze 2996); **71** GR 1772,0319.2 (Bronze 2984); **72** GR 1856,1226.418 (Lamp Q 761); **73** BM (photo P.J. Williams/S. Peckham); **74** GR 1859,0402.102 (Mosaic 45); **75** GR 1946,0514.1; **76** GR 1873,0820.53 (Bronze 1605); **77** GR 1847,0424.19 (Sculpture 1117); **78** TAS; **79** Photo © Roy and Lesley Adkins; **80** GR 1894,1030.1 (Bronze 2695); **81** PE 1857,0806.1; **82** GR 1805,0703.337 (Terracotta D 627); **83** GR 1907,1020.2; **84** BM (photo P.J. Williams/S. Peckham); **85** GR 1805,0703.451 (Sculpture 2448); **86** GR 1907,0518.8–10 (Terracotta 2383–5); **87** Photo © Robert Harding World Imagery; **88** GR 1887,0212.2 (Terracotta C 547), GR 1824,0414.1 (Bronze 1782), GR 1873,0820.591 (Terracotta D 214) (photos N.H. Ramage); **89** GR 1865,0103.36 (Bronze 909); **90** PE 1993,0401.1; **91** GR

1899,0215.1 (Painting 23); **92** GR 1857,1220.414 (Mosaic 54c); **93** PE 1946,1007.1; **94** PE 1978,0102.1; **95** GR 1927,1212.1; **96** CM BMC 1298; **97** GR 1805,0703.301 (Terracotta D 603); **98** GR 1857,1220.440 (Mosaic 51a); **99** Photo © Roy and Lesley Adkins; **100** BM (photo P.J. Williams/S. Peckham); **101** BM (photo P.J. Williams/S. Peckham); **102** GR 1814,0704.213 (Lamp Q 3456); **103** GR 1894,0507.1 (Bronze 788); **104** GR 1865,0712.18 (Bronze 1523); **105** GR 1846,0507.1 (Sculpture 1722) (photo N.H. Ramage); **106** GR 1825,0613.1 (Sculpture 1720); **107** GR 1964,0721.1; **108** GR 1805,0703.51 (Sculpture 1525); **109** GR 1805,0703.11 (Sculpture 1545); **110** Courtesy Sardis Expedition; **111** PE 1965,0409.1; **112** PE 1866,1229.1; **113** Photo © Robert Harding World Imagery; **114** TAS; **115** Photo © Roy and Lesley Adkins; **116** GR 1772,0320.236 (Terracotta D 708); **117** Photo N.H. Ramage; **118** GR 1883,0717.1 (Bronze 1922); **119** GR 1772,0317.21; **120** GR 1856,1226.999 (Lamp Q 3897, Bronze 2547); **121** GR 1926,0216.127 (Lamp Q 3039); **122** GR 1856,1226.1086; **123** Photo © Roy and Lesley Adkins; **124** GR 1757,0815.25A (Bronze 1574); **125** GR 1805,0703.143 (Sculpture 2307); **126** GR 1875,0309.22; **127** GR 1914,0902.3; **128** GR 1904,0204.1168; **129** GR 1917,0601.2749 (Jewellery 2749); **130** GR 1975,0902.6 (Bronze 902); **131** GR 1888,0920.72–8; **132** GR 1872,0405.173; **133** GR 1964,0107.32; **134** GR 1856,1226.422; **135** PE 1881,0626.9; **136** GR 1989,0322.1; **137** PE 1994,0408.33; **138** PE 1994,0408.62–80; **139** GR 1910,1012.1; **140** GR 1865,0103.3 (Sculpture 629); **141** GR 1968,0626.1 (rectal speculum); **142** GR 1865,1118.119 (womb), GR 1839,0214.54 (breast), GR 1865,1118.135 (ear), GR 1865,1118.129 (eye); **143** ME 125204; **144** Photo © Ruggero Vanni/Corbis; **145** GR 1824,0407.10 (Bronze 877); **146** GR 1919,1220.1; **147** PE 1870,0402.526; **148** GR 1772,0317.1; **149** GR 1856,1226.1737 (Sculpture 2401); **150** GR 1805,0703.158 (Sculpture 2379); **151** GR 1858,0819.2 (Sculpture 2275); **152** PE 1969,0701.4; **153** GR 1868,0620.32 (Sculpture 1279); **154** Photo N.H. Ramage; **155** GR 1948,0423.1; **156** GR 1805,0703.153 (Sculpture 2317); **157** GR 1947,0714.8; **158** GR 1805,0703.144 (Sculpture 2315); **159** GR 1888,0806.8 (EA 21810); **160** GR 1939,0324.211 (EA 65346); **161** GR 1994,0521.13 (EA 74715); **162** GR 1956,0517.1; **163** GR 1864,1021.2 (Sculpture 1886); **164** PE 1887,0307,I.68; **165** GR 1784,0131.5 (Sculpture 2109); **166** GR 1776,1108.2 (Sculpture 1736); **167** PE 1995,0402.1; **168** GR 1805,0703.43 (Sculpture 250); **169** PD 1995,0506.8; **170** © Townley Hall Art Gallery & Museums, Burnley Borough Council (photo © The Bridgeman Art Library); **171** GR 1945,0927.1 (Gem 4036); **172** GR 2003,0507.1; **173** GR 1999,0426.1; **174** PE 1988,1208.1; **175** GR 1861,1127.23 (Sculpture 1381); **176** GR 1879,0712.13 (Sculpture 2009); **177** GR 1805,0703.79 (Sculpture 1874); **178** GR 2001,1010.1; **179** © Paris, Musée de l'Armée (Ea 89/1), Dist. RMN (photo © Pascal Segrette); **p. 184** GR 1911,0901.1, PE 1965,1201.1, GR 1850,0304.35 (Sculpture 1890), GR 1874,0712.11 (Sculpture 1893); **p. 185** PE 1848,1103.1, GR 1861,1127.15 (Sculpture 1464), GR 1805,0703.102 (Sculpture 1917); **p. 186** GR 1857,1220.414 (Mosaic 54c).

Select List of Rulers

VESPASIAN

Period	Dynasty/Ruler	Dates Ruled
Etruscan	Tarquin the Proud (Tarquinius Superbus), last king of the Etruscans	535–510 BC
Greek	Alexander the Great	336–323 BC
Roman Republic	Julius Caesar	49–44 BC
Roman Empire	Augustus	27 BC –AD 14
	Julio-Claudians	
	Tiberius	AD 14–37
	Gaius (Caligula)	AD 37–41
	Claudius	AD 41–54
	Nero	AD 54–68
	Flavians	
	Vespasian	AD 69–79
	Titus	AD 79–81
	Domitian	AD 81–96
	(no dynasty name)	
	Nerva	AD 96–8
	Trajan	AD 98–117
	Hadrian	AD 117–38
	Antonines	
	Antoninus Pius	AD 138–61
	Marcus Aurelius	AD 161–80
	Lucius Verus	AD 161–9
	Commodus	AD 180–92
	Severans	
	Septimius Severus	AD 193–211
	Caracalla	AD 211–17
	Elagabalus	AD 218–22
	Alexander Severus	AD 222–35

AUGUSTUS

TRAJAN

CLAUDIUS

Period	Dynasty/Ruler	Dates Ruled
Roman Empire	*Soldier emperors*	
	Maximinus Thrax	AD 235–8
	Balbinus	AD 238
	Philip the Arab	AD 244–9
	Trebonianus Gallus	AD 251–3
	Gallienus	AD 253-268
	Aurelian	AD 270-75
	Tetrarchs	
	Diocletian	AD 284–305
	Maximian	AD 286–305
	Constantius Chlorus	AD 305–6
	Galerius	AD 305–11
	Maxentius	AD 306–12
	Licinius	AD 307–24
	Constantine I, the Great	AD 307–37
	Late Roman emperors	
	Constantius II	AD 337–60
	Julian the Apostate	AD 360–63
	Theodosius I	AD 379–95
	Arcadius [Eastern half of the empire]	AD 395–408
	Honorius [Western half of the empire]	AD 395–423

MARCUS AURELIUS

HADRIAN

CARACALLA

Roman deity	Greek deity	Influence
Aesculapius	Asklepios	Medicine
Apollo; Sol	Apollo	Sun
Bacchus	Dionysos	Wine
Ceres	Demeter	Grain
Cupid	Eros	Love
Cybele	Kybele	Great Mother
Diana; Luna	Artemis	Hunt; Moon
Hercules	Herakles	Strong man
Juno	Hera	Childbirth, Marriage
Jupiter	Zeus	Thunder
Lar		Household
Mars	Ares	War
Mercury	Hermes	Messenger
Minerva	Athena	Wisdom
Neptune	Poseidon	Sea
Pluto	Hades	Underworld
Proserpina	Persephone	Underworld
Silvanus		Woodlands
Vesta	Hestia	Hearth
Venus	Aphrodite	Love
Vulcan	Hephaistos	Metalworking

BACCHUS

GREAT BRITAIN
Bath
Roman Baths and Pump Room
www.romanbaths.co.uk
Cambridge
Fitzwilliam Museum
www.fitzmuseum.cam.ac.uk
Museum of Classical Archaeology,
University of Cambridge
www.classics.cam.ac.uk/museum
Glasgow
Hunterian Museum
www.hunterian.gla.ac.uk
London
British Museum
www.britishmuseum.org
Newcastle
Museum of Antiquities, University
of Newcastle-on-Tyne
www.museums.ncl.ac.uk
Oxford
Ashmolean Museum
www.ashmolean.org
St Albans
Verulamium Museum
www.stalbansmuseums.org.uk

ALGERIA
Algiers
National Museum of Antiquities

AUSTRIA
Vienna
Kunsthistorisches Museum
www.khm.at
Ephesus Museum

CANADA
Montreal
Montreal Museum of Fine Arts
www.mmfa.qc.ca
Ottawa
University of Ottawa Museum of
Classical Antiquities
*www.cla-srs.uottawa.ca/eng/
musee_greco.html*
Toronto
Royal Ontario Museum
www.rom.on.ca

DENMARK
Copenhagen
Ny Carlsberg Glyptotek
www.glyptoteket.dk

FRANCE
Arles
Musée de l'Arles et de la Provence
antiques
www.arles-antique.cg13.fr
Lyon
Musée de la civilisation Gallo-
Romaine
Paris
Louvre Museum
*http://www.louvre.fr/llv/commun/
home.jsp?bmLocale=en*

GERMANY
Berlin
Pergamon Museum
*www.smb.spkberlin.de/smb/standorte
/index.php?lang=en&p=2&objID=27*
Altes Museum
Cologne
Römisch-Germanisches Museum
*www.museenkoeln.de/english/
roemisch-germanisches-museum*
Mainz
Römisch-Germanisches
Zentralmuseum
www.rgzm.de/149.0.html
Munich
Glyptothek
*www.antike-am-koenigsplatz.
mwn.de/glyptothek* (German)
Trier
Rheinisches Landesmuseum
www.rlmb.lvr.de (German)

GREECE
Athens
National Archaeological Museum
of Athens
Benaki Museum
www.benaki.gr
Heraklion
Archaeological Museum
Thessaloniki
Archaeological Museum of
Thessaloniki
www.amth.gr/en/indexen.html

ISRAEL
Jerusalem
Israel Museum
www.english.imjnet.org.il

ITALY
Baia
Castello di Baia

Bologna
Museo Archeologico di Bologna
www.comune.bologna.it/
museoarcheologico
Ferrara
Museo Archeologico di Ferrara
www.archeobo.arti.beniculturali.it/
Ferrara/index.htm
Florence
Museo Archeologico di Firenze
Naples
Museo Archeologico Nazionale di
Napoli
Rome
Musei Capitolini
Musei Vaticani
Museo Nazionale Romano
Villa Giulia Museum
Barracco Museum
Museo della Civiltà Romana
Venice
Museo Archeologico

JORDAN
Amman
National Archaeological Museum

LEBANON
Beirut
National Museum

LIBYA
Tripoli
National Antiquities Museum

NETHERLANDS
Amsterdam
Allard Pierson Museum
www.allardpiersonmuseum.nl/
Leiden
Rijksmuseum van Oudheden
info@rmo.nl

RUSSIA
Moscow
Pushkin Museum of Fine Arts
www.museum.ru/gmii/defengl.htm
St Petersburg
State Hermitage Museum
www.hermitagemuseum.org/
html_En/index.html

SPAIN
Barcelona
Archaeological Museum of Barcelona

Madrid
Museo del Prado
www.museodelprado.es/
National Archaeological Museum
Merida
Museo Nacional de Arte Romano
http://museoarteromano.mcu.es/
index.html
Seville
Archaeological Museum of Seville
www.sevilla5.com/monuments/
arqueologico.html
Tarragona
Museo Nacional Arqeologic de
Tarragona
Zaragoza
Museo del Foro de Caesaraugusta

SYRIA
Damascus
Damascus National Museum

SWITZERLAND
Augst
Römermuseum
www.augusta-raurica.ch
Basel
Antikenmuseum Basel
www.antikenmuseumbasel.ch

TUNISIA
Tunis
Bardo

TURKEY
Antioch
Hatay Archaeological Museum
Aphrodisias
Aphrodisias Museum
Ephesus
Archaeological Museum
Istanbul
Archaeological Museum
Izmir
Archaeological Museum

UNITED STATES
Ann Arbor, MI
Kelsey Museum of Archaeology
www.lsa.umich.edu/kelsey
Atlanta, GA
Michael C. Carlos Museum, Emory
University
www.carlos.emory.edu
Boston, MA
Museum of Fine Arts Boston
www.mfa.org

Cambridge, MA
Arthur M. Sackler Museum
www.artmuseums.harvard.edu/sackler
Chicago, IL
The Art Institute
www.artic.edu/aic
The Oriental Institute
www.oi.uchicago.edu/museum
Cincinnati, OH
Cincinnati Art Museum
www.cincinattiartmuseum.org
Corning, NY
Corning Museum of Glass
www.cmog.org
Cleveland, OH
Cleveland Museum of Art
www.clevelandart.org
Columbia, MO
Museum of Art and Archaeology, the
University of Missouri-Columbia
www.maa.missouri.edu
Detroit, MI
Detroit Institute of Arts
www.dia.org
Kansas City, MO
Nelson-Atkins Museum of Art
www.nelson-atkins.org
Los Angeles, CA
Los Angeles County Museum of Art
www.lacma.org
Minneapolis, MN
The Minneapolis Institute of Arts
www.artsmia.org
New York, NY
Metropolitan Museum of Art
www.metmuseum.org
Brooklyn Museum
www.brooklynmuseum.org
Philadelphia, PA
University of Pennsylvania Museum
of Archaeology and Anthropology
www.museum.upenn.edu
Richmond, VA
Virginia Museum of Fine Arts
www.vmfa.state.va.us
San Francisco, CA
Fine Arts Museums of San Francisco
www.famsf.org
Urbana-Champaign, IL
Krannert Art Museum
www.kam.uiuc.edu
Worcester, MA
Worcester Art Museum
www.worcesterart.org

Index